THE ENDTIME IS NOW
ACCORDING TO THE BIBLE

Revised In Full Color With Detailed Graphs & Charts

BE READY!

C.S. DeCaro

THE ENDTIME IS NOW
ACCORDING TO THE BIBLE

Copyright © 2020 by C.S. DeCaro
All rights reserved. Revised with detailed graphs & charts and grammatical revisions, 2025. Credits & Resources are listed on page 125, and are considered a continuation of the copyright page.

COLOR ILLUSTRATIONS EDITION
& Jesus' Words Red Letter

Also Available: E-Book

BE READY!

Questions Answered & Contradictions Addressed

We are the generation that will have a Complete Understanding of the Endtimes.

> *4"But you, Daniel, shut up the words, and seal the book **until the time of the end**; many shall run to and fro, **and knowledge shall increase**."*
> *Daniel 12:4 NKJV*

> *8 Although I heard, I did not understand. Then I said, "My lord, what shall be the end of these things?" 9 And he said, "Go your way, Daniel, for the words are closed up and sealed **till the time of the end**. 10 Many shall be purified, made white, and refined, but the wicked shall do wickedly; and none of the wicked shall understand, **but the wise shall understand**. Daniel 12:8-10 NKJV*

That time is Now! Be Ready!

In addition to learning how to discern Bible Prophecy, you will also learn:

- The Major Biblical Prophetic events that have already taken place in our recent history since WW1
- The pre-cursors to Biblically foretold imminent events happening now!
- What you need to be Watching for to be prepared for what will happen soon and Jesus' 2nd coming!
- How to BE READY!

This revised full-color version comes 5 years after its original publication. The Daniel 9:27 confirmation of the covenant is on the precipice of beginning. I have not altered any of the original content of this book, except for adding some additional details, timelines, graphs, and grammatical edits. This edition connects all the dots and brings them to life visually! I think you need to understand how we got here and where it's headed. The information in this book is essential for understanding the Biblical prophecies of the last days. We are, in fact, the last generation of Saints that Revelation and other prophetic books are speaking towards. God Bless.

CONTENTS

Introduction: - 9

3 ½ Year Tribulation Not 7 (Principle 1) - - - - - - - - - - - - - 11

Revelation's 4 Accounts of the Second Coming of Jesus
(Principle 2)- 13

United States In The Bible (Principle 3) - - - - - - - - - - - - - - 21

The Seals, Trumpets, and Bowls (Principle 4) - - - - - - - - - 27

Prophetic Timelines - 67

The Antichrist - 71

The False Prophet - 85

The Great Revival & Rapture! - 95

Be Ready! - 117

A Word From The Author - 121

Bibliography - 125

Introduction

Several years ago in my Sunday school class, we did a thorough study of the book of Revelation, verse by verse and chapter by chapter. This study presented a side-by-side comparison of the four main beliefs regarding the rapture of the Church: Pre-tribulation, Mid-Tribulation, Post-Tribulation, and Preterist. This study, however, was skewed towards a Pre-Trib view. Since childhood, I had always believed in a pre-tribulation rapture. To sum it up, I was left with more questions than answers after this study. It seemed they all had flawed views and some unanswerable questions. When I challenged those for a better understanding of specific issues, the response I received was one of an "opinion" or "most logical explanation." This kind of response was not satisfying enough for me. It seemed that the Bible had to have a clear message on the topic of endtimes or eschatology. There were too many contradictions in our Sunday school study that didn't make sense. Every view seemed to try to make the Bible fit into what they wanted it to be. In turn, this created big holes in their arguments.

After this class, I set out to find answers on my own through research and studying the Bible unfiltered, without the predetermined view instilled in me since childhood.

My primary purpose in writing this book is to prepare the Church for what lies ahead with a strong foundational understanding of endtimes. Additionally, I aim to offer genuine Biblical answers to those seeking guidance on how to prepare during these uncertain times. I feel the Church will have to reconcile with all these various, flawed traditional views. There will be a time coming very soon when the Church will be looked upon for answers to some undeniable events on a Biblical proportion, and "opinions" and "most logical explanations" will not be sufficient.

The Bible provides us with clear answers without contradiction. As we walk through these prophetic passages, I will outline four basic principles to help you discern Bible prophecy. Once you grasp these principles, reading books like Daniel and Revelation becomes easier to understand. My goal is to equip you in a way so that when you navigate prophetic passages anywhere in the Bible, you will have some handles to apply when discerning what these powerful passages have to say. It's here folks! The Endtime is Now, Be Ready!

3 ½ Year Tribulation Not 7
(Principle 1)

Traditional belief passed down for years is that the Great Tribulation is seven years. However, there is not one scripture that supports this. Six scriptures say the Great Tribulation will last 3 1/2 years. (*Daniel 7:24-25*) says a different horn (antichrist) will make war with the saints for a time, times, and half a time.

> *24 The ten horns are ten kings*
> *Who shall arise from this kingdom.*
> *And another shall rise after them;*
> *He shall be different from the first ones,*
> *And shall subdue three kings.*
> *25 He shall speak pompous words against the Most High,*
> *Shall persecute the saints of the Most High,*
> *And shall intend to change times and law.*
> *Then the saints shall be given into his hand*
> *For a **time and times and half a time**. Daniel 7:24-25 NKJV*

This is repeated throughout scripture as Time being one year, Times two years, and half a Time is half a year. We know this for sure because the same prophecy is in (*Revelation 13:5*). Here, it says power was given to the Antichrist to continue 42 months (3 1/2 years, Time, Times, ½ Time).

> *5 And he was given a mouth speaking great things and blasphemies, and he was given authority to continue for **forty-two months**. Revelation 13:5 NKJV*

Revelation 12:5-6 says the dragon will make war against the woman (Israel) for 1260 days (3 1/2 years).

> *5 She bore a male Child who was to rule all nations with a rod of iron. And her Child was caught up to God and His throne. 6 Then the woman fled into the wilderness, where she has a place prepared by God, that they should feed her there **one thousand two hundred and sixty days**. Revelation 12:5-6 NKJV*

Here are the other Bible references to a 3 1/2 year tribulation.

> *7 And I heard the man clothed in linen, which was upon the waters of the river, when he held up his right hand and his left hand unto heaven, and sware by him that liveth for ever that it shall be for a **time, times, and half a time**; and when he shall have accomplished to scatter the power of the holy people, all these things shall be finished. Daniel 12:7 NKJV*

> *1 And there was given me a reed like unto a rod: and the angel stood, saying, Rise, and measure the temple of God, and the altar, and them that worship therein. 2 But the court which is without the temple leave out, and measure it not; for it is given unto the Gentiles: and the holy city shall they tread under foot **forty and two months**. 3 And I will give power unto my two witnesses, and they shall prophesy **a thousand two hundred and threescore days**, clothed in sackcloth.*
> Revelation 11:1-3 NKJV

> *14 And to the woman were given two wings of a great eagle, that she might fly into the wilderness, into her place, where she is nourished for a **time, and times, and half a time**, from the face of the serpent. Revelation 12:14 NKJV*

To conclude, Jesus says in *(Matthew 24:15-21)* that when you see the abomination of desolation, let those who be in Judea flee because then shall there be great tribulation such as never has been before nor ever again shall be.

> *15"Therefore when you see the **'abomination of desolation**,' spoken of by Daniel the prophet, standing in the holy place" (whoever reads, let him understand)……..21 For then there will be **great tribulation**, such as has not been since the beginning of the world until this time, no, nor ever shall be.*
> Matthew 24:15, 21 NKJV

Jesus clearly states that the abomination of desolation is the event that will ignite the great tribulation.

We know from *(Daniel 9:27)* that the abomination of desolation will occur at the midpoint of the final seven-year period, referred to as Daniel's 70th week.

> *27 Then he shall confirm a covenant with many for one week; **But in the middle of the week** He shall bring an end to sacrifice and offering. And on the wing of **abominations shall be one who makes desolate,** Even until the consummation, which is determined, **Is poured out on the desolate."***
> Daniel 9:27 NKJV

Jesus says this is the event that ignites the great tribulation, the one spoken of by Daniel the prophet. The first 3 1/2 years of Daniel's 70th week will not be the great tribulation; it doesn't start until the mid-point. This proof also eliminates the possibility of a mid-tribulation rapture theory since that theory is based on a seven-year tribulation. This leaves the pre-trib or post-trib views as the only viable option for the rapture of the Church. As we continue our study, you will see that having a correct understanding of this one simple principle contributes significantly to a clearer understanding of other Bible prophecies.

Revelation 4 Accounts of the 2nd Coming of Jesus
(principle 2)

A great deal of confusion arises for most when trying to understand the book of Revelation. A couple of reasons for this are, for one, they try to compare the Seals, Trumpets, and Bowls as being chronological events all confined within a seven-year timeline. This is a big mistake that we will touch on later in a whole section of its own (Principle 4). However, another reason people have trouble understanding the book of Revelation is that it's actually broken down into four separate accounts of the 2nd coming of Jesus. Once you know this, Revelation becomes much easier to read.

Much like the four books of the New Testament —Matthew, Mark, Luke, and John — provide four separate accounts of Jesus' ministry, death, burial, and resurrection. The book of Revelation also provides us with four accounts from different angles and developments on the culmination of events that lead to the rapture and the Second Coming of Jesus.

Revelation comes from the Greek word Apocalypses, which means the revealing or the unveiling. The topic of the book of Revelation is found in *(Revelation 1:7)*.

> *7 Behold, **He is coming with clouds, and every eye will see Him**, even they who pierced Him. And all the tribes of the earth will mourn because of Him. Even so, Amen. Revelation 1:7 NKJV*

The book of Revelation is divided into three sections.

1) The *"the things which thou has seen"* located in chapter 1.
2) The *"things which are"* located in chapters 2 and 3
3) The *"things which shall be hereafter"* chapters 4 - 22

17 And when I saw Him, I fell at His feet as dead. But He laid His right hand on me, saying to me, "Do not be afraid; I am the First and the Last. 18 I am He who lives, and was dead, and behold, I am alive forevermore. Amen. And I have the keys of Hades and of Death. 19 Write the things which you have seen, and the things which are, and the things which will take place after this. *Revelation 1:17-19 NKJV*

Jesus spoke directly to John and wanted John to record *"the things which thou hast seen"* in chapter 1. Jesus also wanted John to record the *"things which are."* John was at his time the overseer of the seven churches. God had specific messages for each of the seven churches he wanted John to share with them. John did so after he was exiled from the Isle of Patmos. Jesus wanted John to record the *"things which shall be hereafter."* This is the most extensive section of the Book of Revelation, spanning chapters 4-22. The prophetic section. This was the section that recorded everything beyond John's present time. There is a common misconception that the Church is not mentioned beyond chapter 4, which somehow leads to the conclusion that the Church is raptured before any of the events between chapters 4 and 22. This is a significant misunderstanding of God's word, particularly in the book of Revelation, which can lead to misinterpretation of other primary prophetic scriptures, such as Daniel and Jesus' own words in Matthew 24, among others. The Church is actually mentioned numerous times after Chapter 4 of Revelation. Something I look forward to showing you later on in this book.

> *1 After this I looked, and, behold, a door was opened in heaven: and the first voice which I heard was as it were of a trumpet talking with me; which said, Come up hither, and I will shew thee things which must be hereafter.*
> *Revelation 4:1 KJV*

Three of the four accounts of Jesus' 2nd coming are given through the 7 Seals, 7 Trumpets, and 7 Bowls. All of which culminate at the rapture and the 2nd coming of Jesus Christ.

- **The First account** of Jesus' second coming is in the 6th and 7th Seals. *(Revelation 6:12-17 and Revelation 8:5)*

  > *12 I looked when He opened the sixth seal, and behold, there was a* **great earthquake***; and the* **sun became black as sackcloth of hair***, and the* **moon became like blood***. 13 And the* **stars of heaven fell to the earth***, as a fig tree drops its late figs when it is shaken by a mighty wind. 14* **Then the sky receded as a scroll** *when it is rolled up, and* **every mountain and island was moved out of its place***. 15 And the kings of the earth, the great men, the rich men, the commanders, the mighty men, every slave and every free man, hid themselves in*

> the caves and in the rocks of the mountains, 16 and said to the mountains and rocks, "Fall on us and hide us from the face of Him who sits on the throne and from the wrath of the Lamb! 17 **For the great day of His wrath has come**, and who is able to stand?" Revelation 6:12-17 NKJV

> 5 Then the angel took the censer, filled it with fire from the altar, and threw it to the earth. And there were **noises, thunderings, lightnings, and an earthquake**. Revelation 8:5 NKJV

What things happen during the 6th and 7th Seals?

A great earthquake, the sun becomes dark, the moon becomes like blood, stars fall from heaven, the heavens open up, mountains and islands move out of their places, the Day of the Lamb (Jesus) wrath has come, noises, thunders, lightnings, and an earthquake.

- **The Second account** of Jesus' 2nd coming is found in the 7th Trumpet.

(Revelation 11:15-17) Shows us the 2nd coming of Jesus to the earth and setting up his kingdom to rule over all kingdoms. This will be the beginning of the 1,000-year reign.

> 15 Then the seventh angel sounded: And there were **loud voices** in heaven, saying, **"The kingdoms of this world have become the kingdoms of our Lord and of His Christ, and He shall reign forever and ever!"** 16 And the twenty-four elders who sat before God on their thrones fell on their faces and worshiped God, 17 saying: "We give You thanks, O Lord God Almighty, The One who is and who was and who is to come, Because You have taken Your great power and reigned. Revelation 11:15-17 NKJV

The events of the 7th Trumpet (Revelation 11:18-19) are much the same as those in the 7th Seal.

> 18 The nations were angry, and **Your wrath has come**,
> And the time of the dead, that they should be judged,
> And that You should reward Your servants the prophets and the saints, And those who fear Your name, small and great,
> And should destroy those who destroy the earth."
> 19 Then the **temple of God was opened in heaven**, and the ark of His covenant was seen in His temple. And there were **lightnings, noises, thunderings, an earthquake, and great hail**. Revelation 11:18-19 NKJV

What do we find here:

Sounding of the Trumpet, Earthly reign of Jesus begins, Heavens open up, The Day of Jesus' wrath has come, Lightning, Voices, Thunderings, a great earthquake, and Hail.

- **The 2 Harvest is the third account** of Jesus' second coming.

Jesus gave a parable of the 2 harvests in Matthew chapter 13.

> 30 *Let both grow together until the harvest, and at the time of harvest **I will say to the reapers**, "First gather together the **tares** and bind them in bundles to burn them, but gather the **wheat** into my barn." Matthew 13:30 NKJV*

The two harvests are mentioned again in *(Revelation 14:14-20)*

> 14 Then I looked, and behold, **a white cloud, and on the cloud sat One like the Son of Man,** having on His head a golden crown, and in His hand a sharp sickle. 15 And another angel came out of the temple, crying with a loud voice to Him who sat on the cloud, "Thrust in Your sickle and **reap**, for the time has come for You to reap, **for the harvest of the earth is ripe.**" 16 **So He who sat on the cloud thrust in His sickle on the earth, and the earth was reaped.** 17 Then another angel came out of the temple which is in heaven, he also having a sharp sickle. 18 And another angel came out from the altar, **who had power over fire**, and he cried with a loud cry to him who had the sharp sickle, saying, "Thrust in your sharp sickle and gather the clusters of the **vine of the earth**, for her grapes are fully ripe." 19 So the angel thrust his sickle into the earth and gathered the vine of the earth, and threw it into the **great winepress of the wrath of God**. 20 And the winepress was trampled outside the city, and blood came out of the winepress, up to the horses' bridles, for one thousand six hundred furlongs. Revelation 14:14-20 NKJV

The only difference is that the wheat & tares of Matthew are labeled differently. Wheat is called the *"harvest of the earth"*, and the tares are called the harvest of the *"vine of the earth".* (Revelation 14:14-16) is the Rapture, and (verses 17-20) is the wrath of God. Verses 17-20 describe Jesus pouring out his wrath during the Battle of Armageddon.

It doesn't reveal as much detail as the other three accounts. However, we do have:

Loud Voice, the Rapture, the Wrath of God, the Battle of Armageddon

- **The 4th account** of Jesus 2nd coming is found in the 7th Bowl or (Vial) located in *(Revelation 16:15-21)* and continues in *(Revelation 19:6-21)*

15 *"Behold, I am coming as a thief. Blessed is he who watches, and keeps his garments, lest he walk naked and they see his shame."*
16 And they gathered them together to the place called in Hebrew, **Armageddon.** 17 Then the seventh angel poured out his bowl into the air, and a **loud voice** came out of the temple of heaven, from the throne,

saying, **"It is done!"** 18 And there were **noises** and **thunderings and lightnings**; and there was a **great earthquake**, such a mighty and great earthquake as had not occurred since men were on the earth. 19 Now the great city was divided into three parts, and the cities of the nations fell. And great Babylon was remembered before God, to give her the cup of the wine of the **fierceness of His wrath.** 20 Then **every island fled away, and the mountains were not found.** 21 And **great hail** from heaven fell upon men, each **hailstone** about the weight of a talent. Men blasphemed God because of the plague of the hail, since that plague was exceedingly great. Revelation 16:15-21 NKJV

6 And I heard, as it were, **the voice** of a great multitude, as the sound of many waters and as the sound of mighty **thunderings**, saying, "Alleluia! For the **Lord God Omnipotent reigns!** 7 Let us be glad and rejoice and give Him glory, for **the marriage of the Lamb has come**, and His wife has made herself ready." 8 And to her it was granted to be arrayed in fine linen, clean and bright, for the fine linen is the righteous acts of the saints. 9 Then he said to me, "Write: '**Blessed are those who are called to the marriage supper of the Lamb!**' " And he said to me, "These are the true sayings of God." 10 And I fell at his feet to worship him. But he said to me, "See that you do not do that! I am your fellow servant, and of your brethren who have the testimony of Jesus. Worship God! For the testimony of Jesus is the spirit of prophecy." 11 Now **I saw heaven opened**, and behold, a white horse. And He who sat on him was called Faithful and True, and in righteousness He judges and makes war. 12 His eyes were like a flame of fire, and on His head were many crowns. He had a name written that no one knew except Himself. 13 He was clothed with a robe dipped in blood, and His name is called The Word of God. 14 **And the armies in heaven, clothed in fine linen, white and clean, followed Him on white horses.** 15 Now out of His mouth goes a sharp sword, that with it He should strike the nations. And He Himself will rule them with a rod of iron. He Himself treads the **winepress of the fierceness and wrath** of Almighty God. 16 And He has on His robe and on His thigh a name written:

**KING OF KINGS AND
LORD OF LORDS.**

17 Then I saw an angel standing in the sun; and he cried with a **loud voice**, saying to all the birds that fly in the midst of heaven, "Come and gather together for the supper of the great God, 18 that you may eat the flesh of kings, the flesh of captains, the flesh of mighty men, the flesh of horses and of those who sit on them, and the flesh of all people, free and slave, both small and great." 19 And I saw the beast, the kings of the earth, and their armies, gathered together to make war against Him who sat on the horse and against His army. 20.Then the **beast was captured, and with him the false prophet** who worked signs in his presence, by which he deceived those who received the Mark of the Beast and those who worshiped his image. **These two were cast alive into the lake of fire burning with brimstone.** 21 And the rest were killed with the sword which proceeded from the mouth of Him who sat on the horse. And all the birds were filled with their flesh. Revelation 19:6-21 NKJV

We find the same events as in other accounts of Jesus' return;

Armageddon, Loud Voice, Rapture (It Is Done!), Noises, Thunders, Lightnings, Great Earthquake, Islands and Mountains moved out of its place, Great Hail, Marriage of the Lamb, Heavens open up, Those Just Raptured on White horses, Wrath of Jesus, Earthly reign of Jesus begins.

In Revelation chapters 17 and 18, there is an interjection to record the judgment of the one world religion or false religion.

- **There is one more account** outside the book of Revelation by Jesus himself. His disciples asked Jesus a question.

    > 3 Now as He sat on the Mount of Olives, the disciples came to Him privately, saying, **"Tell us, when will these things be? And what will be the sign of Your coming, and of the end of the age?"** Matthew 24:3 NKJV

Jesus continues to answer their question throughout chapter 24, referred to as the Olivet Discourse. Jesus answered their question in great detail about his return in *(Matthew 24:29-31)*.

> 29**"Immediately after the tribulation** of those days the **sun will be darkened, and the moon will not give its light**; the **stars will fall from heaven,** and the powers of the heavens will be shaken. 30**Then the sign of the Son of Man will appear in heaven**, and then all the tribes of the earth will mourn, and they will see the **Son of Man coming on the clouds of heaven with power and great glory.** 31 And He will send His angels with a **great sound of a trumpet,** and **they will gather together His elect from the four winds,** from one end of heaven to the other. Matthew 24:29-31 NKJV

Remember Revelation 1:7 **"Every eye will see him."**

Here is what we see in this account, as presented by Jesus himself.

The sun becomes dark; the moon doesn't give light, stars fall from heaven, the heavens open up, Jesus comes on clouds, a great sound of a trumpet, the Rapture.

All four accounts in Revelation describe the same event with the same attributes. Jesus himself validates these events when answering the disciples' question about his second coming in Matthew 24, with one massive piece of added information. **"Immediately after the tribulation of those days."**

The Bible does not mention Jesus' second coming or the Church's rapture before the Great Tribulation; however, you can find Jesus' own words stating that it will occur immediately after the tribulation.

Something else to remember is that in the 4th account, the 7th bowl. Jesus gives His last warning. Earlier in (Revelation ch. 16), the kings of the earth are gathering down against Israel for the Battle of Armageddon. Jesus pauses to say,

> 15 *"Behold,* ***I am coming as a thief.*** *Blessed is he who watches, and keeps his garments, lest he walk naked and they see his shame." Revelation 16:15 NKJV*

This is the last warning from Jesus before the rapture of the Church. The three verses following Jesus's warning *(Revelation 16:16-18)* are the events at the Battle of Armageddon. Except for one significant prophetic proclamation that comes from the throne of heaven just as the armies gather for battle, **"It is done!"**. I humbly submit to you that this is the climactic point at which the Church's rapture takes place. We will study this further when we get to the section of the seven Bowls.

> *16 And they gathered them together to the place called in Hebrew,* ***Armageddon****.17 Then the seventh angel poured out his bowl into the air, and a* ***loud voice*** *came out of the temple of heaven,* ***from the throne****, saying,* ***"It is done!"*** *18 And there were noises and thunderings and lightnings; and there was a great earthquake, such a mighty and great earthquake as had not occurred since men were on the earth. Revelation 16:16-18 NKJV*

Once you understand that Revelation actually tells the dramatization of events leading to the rapture and 2nd coming of Jesus Christ back to earth from 4 different angles or perspectives, the book doesn't appear to be as confusing to understand as great scholars have made it out to be, making this a fundamental principle to know.

Let's Review

- **1st Account** begins in (Revelation chapter 4 and concludes in Revelation 8:5). The Seven Seals are recorded and end with Jesus's 2nd coming.

- **2nd Account** begins in (Revelation 8:2 through Revelation 11:19). The Trumpets are included in this section. This passage describes many other events leading up to Jesus's return, but concludes again with Jesus's Second Coming and the Rapture.

- **3rd Account** (Revelation chapters 12-14): God reveals more events from yet another perspective, culminating again at Jesus's Second Coming and the Rapture.

- **4th Account** starts over again in (Revelation chapters 15-19). This Account gives us the 7 Bowls. All these events culminate in chapter 19.

Then you have the affirmation of all the accounts by Jesus himself in (Matthew 24:29-31)

United States In The Bible
(Principle 3)

No one will understand the prophecies until the time of the end.

> 8 **Although I heard, I did not understand**. Then I said, "My lord, what shall be the end of these things?"
> 9 And he said, "Go your way, Daniel, for the words are closed up and **sealed till the time of the end**. Daniel 12:8-9 NKJV

THE 4 BEAST

> 1 In the first year of Belshazzar king of Babylon, Daniel had a dream and visions of his head while on his bed. Then he wrote down the dream, telling the main facts.
> 2 Daniel spoke, saying, "I saw in my vision by night, and behold, the four winds of heaven were stirring up the Great Sea. 3 And **four great beasts came up from the sea**, each different from the other. Daniel 7:1-3 NKJV

Many scholars have taught that the four beasts represent: the **lion** as Babylon, the **bear** as Media-Persia, the **leopard** as Greece, and the **ten-horned** kingdom as Rome. This has traditionally been a commonly accepted explanation of this prophecy. However, in *(Daniel 8:20-21)*, it says the ram is Media Persia, and the goat is Greece.

> 20 **The ram** which you saw, having the two horns—they **are the kings of Media and Persia**. 21 And the male **goat is the kingdom of Greece**..... Daniel 8:20-21 NKJV

The kingdoms of Babylon and Media-Persia no longer exist. Daniel chapter 7 states that all of these kingdoms will exist during the time of the Second Coming of Jesus.

Another proof is that the four beasts that Daniel is referring to must arise after Christ's birth; this is found in *(Revelation chapters 12-14)*. This is a single account that we mentioned in Principle 2, which starts with Jesus' birth and concludes at His Second Coming. Jesus was born after the ancient civilizations of Babylon, Media & Persia, and Greece. The Lion, Bear, and Leopard are kingdoms that arise after Jesus' birth but before His Second Coming. Seminaries often attempt to demonstrate that Daniel, chapter 7, mirrors Daniel, chapter 2, Nebuchadnezzar's dream. This is entirely off base, and if you believe this, you will be way off in your foundational understanding of the end times and the book of Revelation. I will cover this more in the section *"The Antichrist."*

We don't have to guess what the four beasts represent. Daniel 7:17, 23 makes it clear that they represent kingdoms or nations, as well as the rulers of these nations.

> 17 'Those **great beasts**, which are four, **are four kings** which arise out of the earth.
>
> 23 "Thus he said:
> 'The **fourth beast** shall be
> A **fourth kingdom on earth**,
> Which shall be different from all other kingdoms,
> And shall devour the whole earth,
> Trample it and break it in pieces. Daniel 7:17, 23 NKJV

We also know that these four beasts represent the kingdoms that will exist during the time of the end of human government and the transition to the kingdom of God. Therefore, if these beasts are represented today, we know we are the generation of the time of the end.

> 9 "I watched till the **thrones were put in place,**
> And the Ancient of Days was seated;……..Daniel 7:9 NKJV

The Ancient of Days refers to Jesus. This is the end of human government transitioning to a Godly One led by Jesus.

Daniel 7:11 is about the Antichrist.

> 11"I watched then because of the sound of the **pompous words which the horn was speaking**; I watched till the **beast was slain**, and its **body destroyed and given to the burning flame**. Daniel 7:11 NKJV

This passage also parallels *(Revelation 19:20).*

> 20 Then the **beast was captured**, and with him the **false prophet** who worked signs in his presence, by which he deceived those who received the Mark of the Beast and those who worshiped his image. **These two were cast alive into the lake of fire burning with brimstone**. Revelation 19:20 NKJV

> 12 As for the **rest of the beasts,** they had their dominion taken away, yet their lives were prolonged for a season and a time. Daniel 7:12 NKJV

Rest of the beasts (nations). They had their dominion (power) taken away. They will be allowed to live into the millennium. This indicates that Jesus will return during the time of these nations (Beasts).

So who are these 4 Beasts? God picked symbols that have meaning during the endtime.

> 4 The **first was like a lion**, and had **eagle's wings**. I watched till its **wings were plucked off**; and it was lifted up from the earth and made to stand on two feet like a man, and a man's heart was given to it. Daniel 7:4 NKJV

LION - is the official symbol of Great Britain.

Verse 4 also states that eagle's wings were growing out of the lion until Daniel watched the wings plucked off.

EAGLES WINGS- is the Official animal symbol of the United States; furthermore, the United States came from Great Britain (*wings plucked off*).

"made to stand on two feet like a man, and a man's heart was given to it". This can be interpreted as the birth of a nation. Interestingly enough, the United States also has another iconic symbol, Uncle Sam.

Daniel, over 2500 years ago, saw the breaking of the U.S. from Great Britain. The Declaration of Independence!

Another interesting personal observation is that our Independence was declared on 7-4-1776, and this passage is found in Daniel 7:4. This observation doesn't necessarily mean anything, but it is interesting.

In *Daniel 7:5,* we find the Bear.

> 5 "And suddenly another beast, a **second, like a bear**. It was raised up on one side, and had three ribs in its mouth between its teeth. And they said thus to it: 'Arise, devour much flesh!' Daniel 7:5 NKJV

BEAR - is Russia's iconic symbol.

> "After this I looked, and there was another, like a **leopard**, which had on its back four **wings of a fowl**. The beast also had **four heads**, and dominion was given to it. Daniel 7:6 NKJV

4-HEADED LEOPARD with FOWL WINGS

Several factors come into play when determining the 3rd beast.

Germany's animal symbol is a black eagle; however, the eagle symbol has already been used in these prophetic passages to describe, most certainly, the United States. Germany does have a prominent symbol that represents the leopard. Germany's Leopard tanks have been used primarily in European armies since the 1960s to the present day.

Germany has always been at the center of European history. The four heads are the number of times a nation will rise and fall. It also states in *Daniel 7:6* that it has wings of a fowl. Therefore, another kingdom is associated with it.

The four heads are the 4 Reichs.

1. Holy Roman Empire of (962-1806)
2. The German Empire (1871-1918), the end of WW1
3. Adolf Hitler's Rule (1933-1945) ended at WW2
4. It seems to be rising today through the European Union, controlled by Germany & France.

The Wings of the Fowl- This nation's official emblem belongs to France, the Rooster.

France and Germany- (the Franco-German Alliance) have been working together since World War II, a collaboration that has led to the establishment of the European Union today.

> 7 "After this I saw in the night visions, and behold, a **fourth beast**, dreadful and terrible, exceedingly strong. It had huge iron teeth; it was devouring, breaking in pieces, and trampling the residue with its feet. It was different from all the beasts that were before it, and **it had ten horns**. Daniel 7:7

The 4th beast is a 10-HORN BEAST

We know from *(Daniel 7:24)* that the 10 horns represent 10 kings (alliance of 10 nations) that shall rule with the Antichrist.

> 24 The **ten horns are ten kings**
> Who shall arise from this kingdom.
> And **another shall rise after them**;
> He shall be different from the first ones, And shall subdue three kings. Daniel 7:24 NKJV

> 23 "Thus he said:
> **'The fourth beast shall be
> A fourth kingdom** on earth,
> Which shall be different from all other kingdoms,
> And **shall devour the whole earth**,
> Trample it and break it in pieces. Daniel 7:23 NKJV

The 4th beast is a picture of a one-world government system. We are watching this system develop today.

So, what will be the role of the United States during the endtime?

If we look at *(Revelation chapter 13)*, we find the four beasts of *(Daniel chapter 7)* mentioned again as a cohesive unit or combo beast. Not in Daniel chapter 2, as seminaries try to teach.

> *1 Then I stood on the sand of the sea. And I saw a beast rising up out of the sea, having seven heads and **ten horns**, and on his horns ten crowns, and on his heads a blasphemous name. 2 Now the beast which I saw was like a **leopard**, his feet were like the feet of a **bear**, and his mouth like the mouth of a **lion**…..Revelation 13:1-2 NKJV*

This is the one-world government led by the Antichrist. One thing you won't find anywhere in Revelation, chapter 13, is the eagles' wings. So, where are the eagles' wings? If you go back to the previous chapter, Revelation chapter 12, it shows us where the eagles' wings are.

> *14 But the woman was given two **wings of a great eagle**, that she might fly into the wilderness to her place, where she is **nourished for a time and times and half a time**, from the presence of the serpent. Revelation 12:14 NKJV*

The United States will be right by Israel's (the woman) side in opposition to the Antichrist and his one-world government throughout the 3 1/2 year tribulation. You may be thinking to yourself, but the Bible says that all nations will come against Jerusalem, as found in Zechariah 14:2. My answer to that is, could it be that what is referenced here is the "United Nations" as "all nations"? After all, who makes the decisions on behalf of all nations now? The "United Nations" can certainly be interpreted as being "all nations."

The United States defending Israel will not be the popular stance in the eyes of the world during the endtime. Antisemitism is growing rapidly globally now. Still, it's always better to stand with God than Satan *(Genesis 12:3)*. Presently, the U.S. has been more supportive of Israel than at any other time in history, not to mention that the U.S. has pulled out of several world government entities these past few years, with the World Health Organization being the latest at the time of this writing. Also, I would like to add that the United Nations has passed more sanctions against Israel than any other nation on the planet, bar none. The United States has been vetoing just about all of them in defense of Israel. Regardless of the future administrations and the direction they may take the United States in terms of policies, the Bible prophecies always come to pass. The United States (Eagles Wings) will defend Israel throughout the 3 1/2 year tribulation.

In conclusion, correctly understanding Daniel's four beasts is crucial for comprehending other Biblical prophecies. This is a must-know Principle.

33 And they that understand among the people shall instruct many…Daniel 11:33 NKJV

The SEALS, TRUMPETS, and BOWLS
(principle 4)

First, there is a misconception that these three groups of seven all take place during the tribulation period and sometimes refer to the same events during that time. This is why there is so much confusion and contradictions among scholars when interpreting these three groups, which again leads to a domino effect of misinterpreting everything else in the book of Revelation. John wasn't writing about events that would only take place during the final seven years; however, he was writing about future events that would occur beyond his present time until the Rapture of the Church and Christ's Second Coming. Nowhere in Revelation does it state that the events spoken of by John are limited to the final seven years only.

This is a large section but critical to understanding the book of Revelation. So let's jump in. Three primary groups of seven are found in Revelation: the 7 Seals, the 7 Trumpets, and the 7 Bowls (also referred to as Vials). These comprise the skeletal framework of the book of Revelation. The 7 Seals are the long story that ends at the 2nd coming of Jesus and the Battle of Armageddon. The 7 Trumpets is the shorter story that ends at the 2nd coming of Jesus and the Battle of Armageddon. The 7 Bowls are a very brief story that concludes with the 2nd coming of Jesus and the Battle of Armageddon. We are presently amid the 7 Seals and the 7 Trumpets, which are already being unveiled. The 7 Bowls don't occur until after the Mark of the Beast is doled out. We know this since when the first bowl is poured out, the Bible makes very clear that it will be unleashed upon the individuals who have taken the Mark of the Beast. (Revelation 16:2)

> *2 So the **first** went and poured out his **bowl** upon the earth, and a foul and loathsome sore **came upon the men who had the mark of the beast** and those who worshiped his image. Revelation 16:2 NKJV*

So from that reference, we know that the seven Bowls don't begin until the very end.

The Book of Revelation also includes parenthetical chapters. When we correctly understand the skeletal structure of the Seven Seals, Seven Trumpets, and Seven Bowls, we will gain a deeper understanding of the other chapters as well; this will provide a comprehensive view and a fuller understanding of what all of this means.

THE 7 SEALS

Begins in *(Revelation 6:1)* through *(Revelation 8:5)*

The term "Seal" is derived from the tradition of placing a seal on specified files or documents that prevents anyone from reviewing the files without receiving a court order from a judge. Here in Revelation, the term 'Seal' is not the first time it has been used; remember, Daniel was told in Daniel 12 that the words he wrote would be sealed until the time of the end, and only the wise would understand. Also, God told John in Revelation chapter 10 to seal up the things which the seven thunders uttered, and not to write them. Here in Revelation, Jesus is simply revealing information to us that would only be understood during the time of the end for our benefit. Because these are Seals, Jesus, as the Judge, is the only one who can open the seals. This is why the Lamb of God is mentioned in every Seal that is opened. You can read about this further in the previous chapter, Revelation 5.

The first 4 Seals are the four horsemen of the Apocalypse. Many books, movies, and commentaries have been made about these four horsemen of the Apocalypse. Today, I want to bring to light who these four horsemen of the Apocalypse are. Let's look at *Revelation 6:1-8.*

1st Seal is the White Horse
2nd Seal is the Red Horse
3rd Seal is the Black Horse
4th Seal is the Pale Horse

*1 And I saw when **the Lamb** opened one of the seals, and I heard, as it were the noise of thunder, one of the four beasts saying, Come and see. 2 And I saw, and behold a **white horse**: and he that sat on him had a bow; and a crown was given unto him: and he went forth conquering, and to conquer. 3 And when he had opened the second seal, I heard the second beast say, Come and see. 4 And there went out another **horse that was red**: and power was given to him that sat thereon to take peace from the earth, and that they should kill one another: and there was given unto him a great sword. 5 And when he had opened the third seal, I heard the third beast say, Come and see. And I beheld, and lo a **black horse**; and he that sat on him had a pair of balances in his hand. 6 And I heard a voice in the midst of the four beasts say, A measure of wheat for a penny, and three measures of barley for a penny; and see thou hurt not the oil and the wine. 7 And when he had opened the fourth seal, I heard the voice of the fourth beast say, Come and see. 8 And I looked, and behold a **pale horse**: and his name that sat on him was Death, and Hell followed with him. And power was given unto them over the fourth part of the earth, to kill with sword, and with hunger, and with death, and with the beasts of the earth. Revelation 6:1-8 NKJV*

White Horse *(Revelation 6:1-2)*
Red Horse   *(Revelation 6:3-4)*
Black Horse *(Revelation 6:5-6)*
Pale Horse *(Revelation 6:7-8)*

Most of the book of Revelation is written in symbols; however, as we have already discovered earlier in (Principle 3), these are also meant to be understood. When trying to get a complete understanding of Bible prophecy or anything in scripture, for that matter, it's a good idea to see if other accounts in the Bible can help fill in some answers so that you can get a complete picture by bringing them together.

I say that to say this, there is another account of the four horsemen of the apocalypse written about 600 years before John's account. It's in the Old Testament book of *Zechariah 6:1-8*. Coincidentally, both Zechariah & Revelation accounts are found in chapters 6:1-8. Let's look at Zechariah 6:1-3.

> *1 And I turned, and lifted up mine eyes, and looked, and, behold, there came four chariots out from between two mountains; and the mountains were mountains of brass.*
> *2 In the first chariot were **red horses**; and in the second chariot **black horses**;*
> *3 And in the third chariot **white horses**; and in the fourth chariot **grisled and bay horses**. Zechariah 6:1-3 NKJV*

There are four horsemen in Zechariah as well, but instead are pulling chariots. However, it's the colors that are important! The fourth horse is mentioned as grisled and bay. Both in Zechariah and Revelation, the colors match. These colors are of great significance, so how can we interpret them? Zechariah gives us the big clue. *(Zechariah 6:4-5)*

> *4 Then I answered and said unto the angel that talked with me,* **What are these, my lord?**
> *5 And the angel answered and said unto me,* **These are the four spirits** *of the heavens, which go forth from standing before the Lord of all the earth. Zechariah 6:4-5 NKJV*

What are these horses and their riders? They are four spirits. Interestingly, galloping horses are used to describe these Seals. This is an indication that these four Seals are not one-off events but rather a spirit of influence that will become more prominent as we approach the return of Christ. In other words, these spirits are present and active throughout, until the end of time. The next question would be, what spirits could we associate with White, Red, Black, and Pale? The dots start connecting as you think about spirits that go through nations and influence people to do what they do, and sometimes even cause nations to go to war.

There is an international belief system associated with the color red. It's communism. For example, it's easy to see in Red China, Red Russia, Red Romania, etc....So communism is the Red Spirit putting people under its influence.

The RED HORSE
(Revelation 6:4)

*4 And there went out another horse that was red: and **power was given to him** that sat thereon to **take peace from the earth**, and that they should **kill one another**: and there was given unto him a **great sword**. Revelation 6:4 KJV*

Communism has *"taken peace from the earth"* throughout history. Wherever communism spreads, a revolution follows. Look at China, Russia, Congo, and even during the Hitler era. *"They kill one another,"* history shows in the communist movement; there is a lot of infighting to gain power. The *"great sword"* represents a great military might. Russia and China are military forces with great power. It's because communism has been given a *"great sword."* The 2nd Seal, the Red Horse, is Communism.

The BLACK HORSE *(Revelation 6:5-6)*

*5 And when he had opened the third seal, I heard the third beast say, Come and see. And I beheld, and lo a **black horse**; and he that sat on him had a **pair of balances** in his hand. 6 And I heard a voice in the midst of the four beasts say, A measure of wheat for a penny, and three measures of barley for a penny; and see thou hurt not the oil and the wine. Revelation 6:5-6 KJV*

These symbols associated with the black horse symbolize Capitalism. The rider on the black horse *"had a pair of balances,"* which symbolizes trade and commerce. The capitalist system thrives through business. In verse 6, it refers to the economy of a capitalist system—think of the stock market or supply chain with nations, tariffs, etc.

Capitalism is recognized by Financial, Journalistic, and Diplomatic circles as the black power of today, much like communism, which is known as the red power. The 3rd Seal, the Black Horse, is Capitalism.

God did not use the colors of horses ambiguously without meaning. He wanted to speak to us about Communism & Capitalism. These are their actual colors and meanings!

The WHITE HORSE *(Revelation 6:2)*

*2 And I saw, and behold a **white horse**: and he that sat on him had a bow; and a crown was given unto him: and he went forth conquering, and to conquer. Revelation 6:2 NKJV*

He had a bow with no arrows; however, he went out conquering. Communism, Capitalism, and Catholicism are all powers that are always reaching for power and have been at the center of wars throughout history. The Roman Catholic Church began around 590 AD.

The Pope wears white because it represents holiness; he has always been called Your Holiness. The Pope's helicopter is white, his car is white, and his airplane is white. Five years ago, I wrote in my first edition that if he had a horse, it would probably be white too. Well, folks, Pope Leo XIV was the first Pope to ever acquire a horse on 10/15/2025. Yes, it is white!

Pope Leo XIV was the first Pope to acquire a horse

The power hub of the Pope is concentrated in Vatican City inside Rome, Italy, and is considered a theocracy. The "Holy See" is the name given to the government of the Roman Catholic Church, which the Pope leads as the bishop of Rome. As such, the Holy See's authority extends over Catholics worldwide. Since 1929, it has resided in Vatican City, which was established as an independent state to enable the Pope to exercise his universal authority. On the other hand, the Antichrist will use much military force, as mentioned throughout scripture, Daniel 11:31 states, *"arms shall stand on his part."* This white horse is not the Antichrist.

A crown was given unto him. Originally, Popes didn't wear crowns until around the 8th century, and from then on, Popes have at times worn crowns. Most notable now is the triple crown that took form in the 14th century. Very interesting how dots start connecting. The 1st Seal, the White Horse, is Catholicism.

31

The Endtime Is Now

The PALE HORSE *(Revelation 6:7-8)*

The original Greek word for pale used here is Chloros, which means green or yellowish-green. I've used the New King James Version or the King James Version throughout this study. Interestingly enough, the NRSV or New Revised Standard Version does translate *(Revelation 6:8)* as a pale green horse.

*8 I looked and there was a **pale green horse!** Its rider's name was **Death, and Hades followed with him**; they were given **authority over a fourth of the earth**, to kill with sword, famine, and pestilence, and by the wild animals of the earth. Revelation 6:7-8 NRSV*

Green is the official color of Islam.

The green horse rider is *"death"*. Muhammad believed in killing to further the power of Islam.

Dome of the Rock, Temple Mount, Jerusalem

Graphic Content Warning

There are many suicide bombers and terrorists in Radical Islam, especially in the Middle East. Just look at what happened on October 7th. Their motivation is because the rider on the horse is death. *"Hell follows with him."* They believe the highest thing they can do is die for Allah. In return for martyrdom, they are told they will have immediate access to paradise with 72 virgins. Muslims are taught that the only way they can know for sure of their salvation is to become a martyr for Allah. This is a lie they are told because hell follows with him.

Authority was given to the green horse rider over a *"fourth part of the earth."* According to a 2019 population study, the world's population is currently over 8 billion people. As of 2020, the Pew Research Center suggests there are a total of 2 billion muslims worldwide—precisely one-fourth of the world's population.

The Endtime Is Now

They are to *"kill with the sword"*. Radical Islam is well known today for beheadings. It says they will die of hunger (famine). Over 90% of Muslims live in the southern hemisphere, Africa & Asia is where there is a lot of hunger, and life spans are shortened. The 4th Seal, the Pale Horse, is Islam.

The four colors —White, Red, Black, and Green —match identically with the four belief systems that are vying for the hearts and minds of people on earth today. This prophecy, written 2,000 years ago, utilized the exact colors of the four major belief systems today. It's incredible!

* Catholicism - White
* Communism - Red
* Capitalism - Black
* Islamism - Green

The era of the Green Horse is right now. This also means we are currently just before the 5th Seal!

The 5th Seal SOULS UNDER THE ALTAR *(Revelation 6:9-11)*

> *9 When He opened the **fifth seal**, I saw **under the altar the souls of those who had been slain for the word of God and for the testimony which they held**. 10 And they cried with a loud voice, saying, "How long, O Lord, holy and true, until You judge and avenge our blood on those who dwell on the earth?" 11 Then **a white robe was given to each of them**; and it was said to them that they should rest a little while longer, until both the number of their fellow servants and their brethren, who would be killed as they were, was completed. Revelation 6:9-11*

This depicts the **Great Tribulation** that begins at the 3 1/2 year point. Some Christians will be killed in the Great Tribulation, and their spirits are with God, and they are asking God How long will it be before their blood is avenged upon them still on the earth? God replied that it would be a short time. They are given white robes and will be joined later by a great multitude that *"come out"* (raptured) of the Great Tribulation that will also be wearing white robes.

> *9 After these things I looked, and behold, **a great multitude which no one could number**, of <u>all nations, tribes, peoples, and tongues</u>, standing before the throne and before the Lamb, **clothed with white robes**, with palm branches in their hands... 13 Then one of the elders answered, saying to me, "**Who are these arrayed in white robes, and where did they come from?**" 14 And I said to him, "Sir, you know." So he said to me, "These are the ones who <u>come out of the great tribulation</u>, and washed their robes and made them white in the blood of the Lamb. Revelation 7:9, 13-14*

The 5th Seal is the Great Tribulation period.

The 6th Seal HEAVEN'S DEPART LIKE A SCROLL
(Revelation 6:12-14)

> *12 And I beheld when he had opened the **sixth seal**, and, lo, there was a great earthquake; and the sun became black as sackcloth of hair, and the moon became as blood;*
> *13 And the stars of heaven fell unto the earth, even as a fig tree casteth her untimely figs, when she is shaken of a mighty wind. 14 And **the heaven departed as a scroll** when it is rolled together; and every mountain and island were moved out of their places. Revelation 6:12-14 NKJV*

The Bible teaches that the heavens will depart at the 2nd coming of Jesus to the earth. As you continue to read the following three verses (Revelation 6:15-17), people of all statures try to hide themselves from Jesus and the wrath that he brings.

> *15 And the kings of the earth, and the great men, and the rich men, and the chief captains, and the mighty men, and every bondman, and every free man, **hid themselves in the dens and in the rocks of the mountains;***
> *16 And said to the mountains and rocks, Fall on us, and hide us from the face of him that sitteth on the throne, and from the **wrath of the Lamb**:*
> *17 For the **great day of his wrath is come**; and who shall be able to stand? Revelation 6:15-17 NKJV*

The 6th Seal marks Jesus' second coming to the earth to execute his wrath against the world's nations that rejected him.

The 7th Seal ONE HALF HOUR OF SILENCE *(Revelation 8:1)*

> *1 When He opened the seventh seal, **there was silence in heaven for about half an hour**. Revelation 8:1 NKJV*

The 7th Seal concludes the 2nd coming of Jesus to the earth.

So what is this half-hour of silence? I believe all eyes from heaven are watching this climactic event of the **Marriage Supper of the Lamb**. The gathering of the wheat from the tares has happened. The tares have been left behind in Seal 6 in fear as the world witnessed the harvest of the earth take place. This all occurs at the end of the Great Tribulation, as the nations gather against Israel for the Battle of Armageddon. After this half-hour silence in the sky (Marriage Supper of the Lamb), the Battle of Armageddon has already begun, and half of the city of Jerusalem has been taken. We will come with Jesus on white horses after partaking in the Marriage Supper of the Lamb in the sky as He fights against those nations; His feet will stand once again on earth on the Mount of Olives, not since He was here the first time 2,000 years ago.

Last warning right before the rapture as nations gather at Armageddon.

> *15 "Behold, **I am coming as a thief**. Blessed is he who watches, and keeps his garments, lest he walk naked and they see his shame." 16 And they gathered them together to the place called in Hebrew, **Armageddon**. Revelation 16:15-16*

> *1 Behold, **the day of the Lord is coming,**
> And **your spoil will be divided in your midst**.
> 2 For **I will gather all the nations to battle against Jerusalem**;
> The city shall be taken,
> The houses rifled,
> And the women ravished.
> **Half of the city shall go into captivity**,
> But the remnant of the people shall not be cut off from the city.
> 3 **Then the Lord will go forth**
> **And fight against those nations,**
> **As He fights in the day of battle.**
> 4 And in that day **His feet will stand on the Mount of Olives**..Zechariah 14:1-4*

> *And the **armies in heaven, clothed in fine linen, white and clean, followed Him on white horses**. Revelation 19:14*

Next, the angels were given 7 Trumpets; however, they were not told to blow them yet; they were just given the trumpets.

> *2 And I saw the seven angels who stand before God, and to them were **given seven trumpets**. 3 Then **another angel**, having a golden censer, came and stood at the altar. He was given much incense, that he should offer it with the prayers of all the saints upon the golden altar which was before the throne. 4 And the smoke of the incense, with **the prayers of the saints, ascended before God from the angel's hand.** Revelation 8:2-4 NKJV*

Another note to take from this passage is that your prayers accomplish mighty things and will be answered according to God's timing and His will.

This passage below concludes the 7th Seal.

> *5 Then the angel took the censer, filled it with fire from the altar, and threw it to the earth. **And there were noises, thunderings, lightnings, and an earthquake.**
> Revelation 8:5 NKJV*

I want to take a moment here to show you something. Let's compare the 7th Seal with the 7th Trumpet and 7th Bowl.

7th Trumpet *(Revelation 11:19)*

> *19 Then the **temple of God was opened in heaven**, and the ark of His covenant was seen in His temple. And there were **lightnings, noises, thunderings, an earthquake, and great hail.** Revelation 11:19 NKJV*

7th Bowl *(Revelation 16:17-18)*

> *17 Then the seventh angel poured out his bowl into the air, and **a loud voice came out of the temple of heaven**, from the throne, saying, **"It is done!"** 18 And **there were noises and thunderings and lightnings; and there was a great earthquake,** such a mighty and great earthquake as had not occurred since men were on the earth.*
> *Revelation 16:17-18 NKJV*

We see that the 7th Seal, 7th Trumpet, and 7th Bowl are the **same exact event**.

The Seals are the Long story ending at the Battle of Armageddon and Jesus's second coming. The Trumpets are the shorter story ending at the Battle of Armageddon and Jesus's second coming, and the Bowls are the very short story ending at the Battle of Armageddon and Jesus's second coming.

Next, I will discuss the seven Trumpets. Although it is stated in verse 2 of chapter 8 that John saw the angels with the Trumpets, they didn't start sounding them until after the Seals were finished, as mentioned in verse 5. The Trumpets begin to sound in verse 6. This is an important distinction because the story starts over again from the perspective of the trumpets; it's not a continuation from the Seals that many teach as proof of a chronological order to these three groups. The reason for pointing out the comparisons of the 7th Seal, 7th Trumpet, and 7th Bowl is that it proves conclusively that the book of Revelation is not in chronological order, which, of course, is the basis of the pre-tribulation rapture. This easy comparison brings their whole theory of the book of Revelation being written in Chronological order, crashing down.

The 7 Trumpets

Begins in *(Revelation 8:6)* and concludes in *(Revelation 11:15-19)*

> *6 So the seven angels who had the seven trumpets prepared themselves to sound. Revelation 8:6 NKJV*

The 7 Trumpets are not the same as the 7 Seals. Only the last Trumpet is the same as the last Seal; the others differ. The traditional view of the 7 Trumpets is that all events from chapter 4 of Revelation and following are events that will only happen during the final seven years. However, with the fact that the first four seals have already opened after Revelation chapter 4, we know that this concept is not necessarily true. So, let's take a new look at the 7 Trumpets.

1 Trumpet

> *7 The first angel sounded: And hail and fire followed, mingled with blood, and they were **thrown to the earth**. And a third of the trees were burned up, and all green grass was burned up. Revelation 8:7 NKJV*

During WW1, airplanes first became a part of warfare, and they were literally throwing bombs from planes, fire followed, killing men. Large amounts of artillery shells and chemical agents were used for the first time on troops, killing over 8 million people. Understand, John was witnessing this vision and had never seen things like this before. He was writing what he saw. This verse also talks about the earth and green things being burnt up. It was during WW1 when biological and chemical weapons were first used as battlefield weapons. This all contributed to a policy called the scorched earth policy. The concept was when retreating before the enemy, to ensure not to leave anything useful for them, no vegetation, weapons, etc....Both sides followed this policy, which caused vast amounts of land to be burnt up and vegetation to be destroyed. In WW1, 8.2 million people died. This was the 1st Trumpet.

The Endtime Is Now

2 Trumpet

> *8 Then the second angel sounded: And something like **a great mountain burning with fire was thrown into the sea**, and a third of the sea became blood. 9 And a third of the living creatures in the sea died, and **a third of the ships were destroyed**. Revelation 8:8-9 NKJV*

World War II, 1939 - 1945. Fifty-two million people died in this war. How many ships participated, and how many were sunk? 105,127 ships participated in WW2, and 36,387 were sunk. Almost exactly 1/3. The nuclear bomb deployed at Hiroshima and Nagasaki resembled *"Something like a great mountain burning with fire."* This was the first atomic bomb dropped and was a new sight on the world stage. I've tried to research animal deaths as well as sea animal deaths during wars. I found that tens of thousands of land animals died during these wars, with horses being among the highest numbers. However, it seems impossible to know the number of sea animals' deaths for obvious reasons. We understand the devastation a nuclear fallout can have, and with all the ships at sea waging war against each other, what effect it could have on the sea creatures. I can only say I have no reason to believe this war didn't cause 1/3 of the sea creatures to die because of the fact that the other portions of this prophecy match so perfectly. A third of the ships and a great fire cast into the islands of Japan located out in the sea, WW2 was the 2nd Trumpet.

Atomic Bomb dropped on
Nagasaki August 8, 1945

3rd Trumpet

*10 Then the third angel sounded: And a great star fell from heaven, **burning like a torch**, and it fell on a third of the rivers and on the springs of water. 11The name of the star is **Wormwood**. A third of the **waters became wormwood, and many men died from the water**, because it was made bitter. Revelation 8:10-11 NKJV*

April 26th, 1986, in Ukraine, the "Chernobyl Nuclear Power Plant" exploded, which resulted in the worst nuclear accident in the history of the world. The actual Russian word for "Wormwood" is "Chernobyl." Many people at the time did speculate that the nuclear explosion might indeed be the 3rd Trumpet.

Wormwood is mentioned seven times in the Hebrew Bible, always with the implication of bitterness. The word *Wormwood* appears several times in the Old Testament, translated from the Hebrew term (*la'anah*, which means "curse" in Hebrew). Wormwood is mentioned only once in the New Testament, in the Book of Revelation: Many Bible scholars consider the term *Wormwood* to be a purely symbolic representation of the bitterness that will fill the earth during troubled times, noting that the plant for which Wormwood is named, *Artemisia absinthium*, or Mugwort, *Artemisia vulgaris*, is a known Biblical metaphor for unpalatably bitter things.

Chernobyl Angel blowing 3rd Trumpet, Monument

The Chernobyl Power Plant was located in a town of about 40K people. There were two explosions. The 1st explosion blew an extremely heavy metal concrete lid off the nuclear reactor. The second explosion threw radioactive material about a mile into the air, and the reactor continued to *"burn like a torch."* The cloud of radiation was carried by winds north into Scandinavian countries and then across Europe. The government had to declare an exclusion zone that covered 1,000 square miles in Ukraine. Today, in the city of Pripyat, where most of the power plant workers lived, it is a ghost town. Authorities today say they don't expect the area to be inhabitable for another 100-300 years. Chernobyl was the world's worst nuclear accident!

The Bible says many men died because of the waters. The Nuclear cloud that carried over Europe brought radioactivity to the ground, which caused vast amounts of soil to be contaminated that were referred to as "Brown Outs," where nothing would grow for the next 100 years. Many of Europe's rivers were filled with water from the rain clouds, and those who drank from the streams ingested a nuclide, Cesium-137. This, when ingested, goes into the bone marrow and has a half-life of 30 years. This means that after approximately 30 years of ingestion, cancer can develop. The reason so many people died was because of the water. The prophecy says many men died because of the waters. At the time, about 125K people were already estimated dead; Chernobyl infected around 2 million throughout Europe, so the fallout is still ongoing. Most livestock had to be slaughtered and disposed of; Cesium-137 filled the waters of Europe, and little did the people know that when they drank from these waters, they were ingesting radioactive poison.

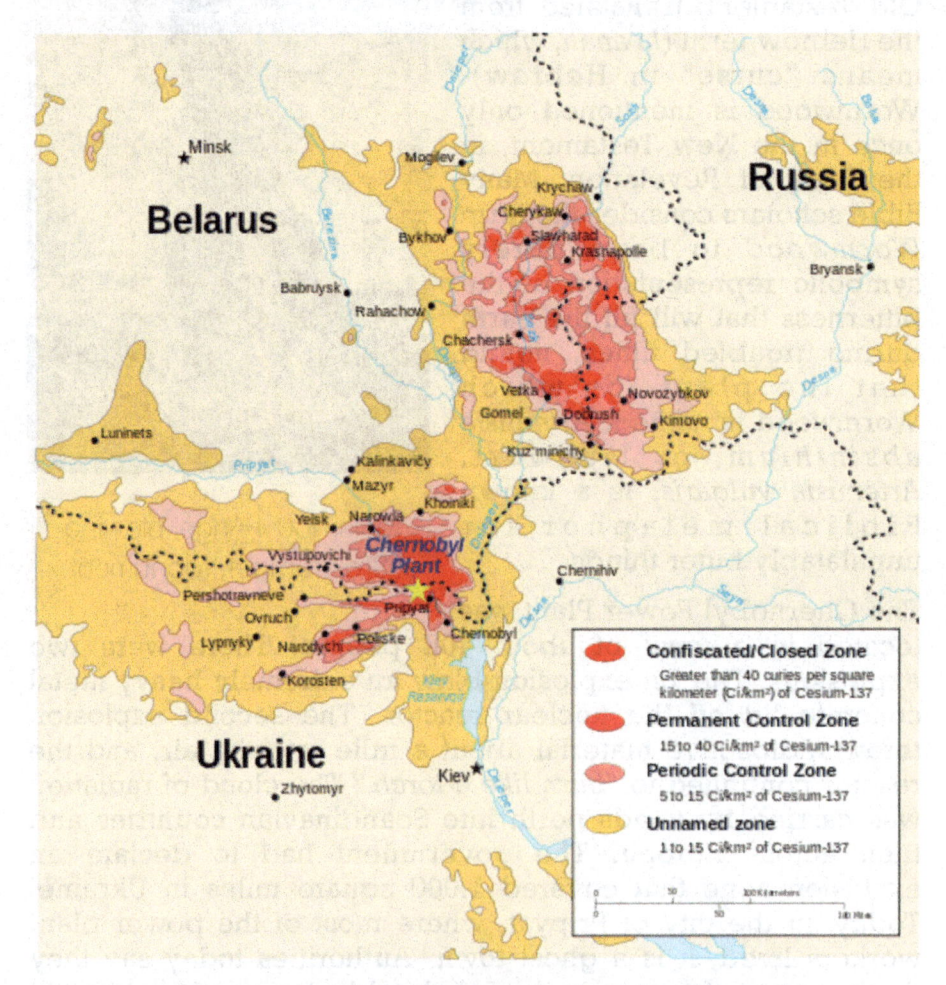

The 3rd Trumpet Sounded on April 26th, 1986.

The 4th Trumpet

> *12 Then the fourth angel sounded: And **a third** of the sun was struck, **a third** of the moon, and **a third** of the stars, so that **a third** of them were darkened. **A third of the day** did not shine, and **likewise the night**. Revelation 8:12 NKJV*

This is the prophecy of the shortening of the days. Jesus also prophesies about the shortening of the days in *Matthew 24:22*.

> *22 And **unless those days were shortened**, no flesh would be saved; but **for the elect's sake those days will be shortened**. Matthew 24:22 NKJV*

So is this saying the number of days will be shortened, or the length of each day is shortened? Let's look at *Daniel 12:11-12*.

> *11"And from the time that the daily sacrifice is taken away, and the abomination of desolation is set up, **there shall be one thousand two hundred and ninety days**. 12 Blessed is he who waits, and comes to the **one thousand three hundred and thirty-five days**. Daniel 12:11-12*

This is a specific prophecy of how long it would be from the abomination of desolation till the end of the reign of the Antichrist and, finally, the establishment of the kingdom of God on the earth.

These days are engraved in God's word; therefore, you can't change the number of days. So, it means the length of each day will be shortened.

How were the days shortened? Things are sped up, and time is moving faster and faster as we continue to approach Christ's return. How?

Don't know if you have ever heard of Einstein's theory of relativity. It states that time and speed are relative to each other. If this is true and time has sped up, what significant event occurred to cause this to happen? On **November 9th, 1989**, the Berlin Wall came down. This was the beginning of the "New World Order," when a new age of globalization began to develop. President Ronald Reagan challenged Mikhail Gorbachev to "tear down this wall!" Twenty-nine months later, **the 4th Trumpet sounded**. We have seen the acceleration of means of organizing politics, economics, the internet, and social life since then

The Endtime Is Now

Let's look at *Revelation 8:13* "The 3 Woes"

> *13 And I looked, and I heard an angel flying through the midst of heaven, saying with a loud voice, "**Woe, woe, woe** to the inhabitants of the earth, because of **the remaining blasts of the trumpet** of the three angels who are about to sound!" Revelation 8:13 NKJV*

These three woes are in reference to the three remaining trumpets, each representing a woe.

The 5th Trumpet (1st Woe)

*Then the **fifth angel sounded**: And I saw a star fallen from heaven to the earth. **To him was given the key to the bottomless pit**. 2 And he opened the bottomless pit, and smoke arose out of the pit like the **smoke of a great furnace**. So the **sun and the air were darkened because of the smoke of the pit**. 3 Then out of the smoke locusts came upon the earth. And to them was given power, as the scorpions of the earth have power. **4 They were commanded not to harm the grass of the earth, or any green thing, or any tree**, but only those men who do not have the seal of God on their foreheads. **5 And they were not given authority to kill them, but to torment them for five months.** Their torment was like the torment of a scorpion when it strikes a man. **6 In those days men will seek death and will not find it; they will desire to die, and death will flee from them.** 7 The shape of the locusts was like horses prepared for battle. On their heads were crowns of something like gold, and their faces were like the faces of men. 8 They had hair like women's hair, and their teeth were like lions' teeth. 9 And they had breastplates like breastplates of iron, and the sound of their wings was like the sound of chariots with many horses running into battle. 10 They had tails like scorpions, and there were stings in their tails. Their power was to hurt men five months. 11 And they had as <u>**king**</u> over them the <u>**angel of the bottomless pit**</u>, whose name in Hebrew is Abaddon, but in Greek he has the name Apollyon. 12 One woe is past. Behold, still two more woes are coming after these things. Revelation 9:1-12 NKJV*

According to prophecy, the fifth Trumpet will sound before a bottomless pit of fire that causes massive amounts of smoke to block the light of the sun. This person has access to the pit to open it up. Saddam Hussein invaded Kuwait in 1990. In what was known as the first Gulf War. President Bush ordered Saddam to withdraw from Kuwait; in frustration, Saddam Hussein set fire to **over 700 oil wells.**

The fires in Kuwait were videoed. Pictures taken at noon showed everything blackened as if it were midnight in Kuwait due to the black smoke emitted by the oil wells on fire. For several months, they did not see the sun or sky from Kuwait.

Prophecy also says locusts came out of the smoke but were ordered not to harm the vegetation, only the men *(Revelation 9:3-9)*. By this time, we've developed more advanced military weapons that were able to combat in a more precisely targeted method with minimal collateral damage, unlike WWI or WWII. Now John is seeing this in his vision and attempting to describe things he's never seen before. Jet airplanes, helicopters, and tanks. Breastplates of iron, faces of men, and hair of women. Helicopters look a lot like a locust. If you have never seen Jet airplanes or helicopters in your life, and now you see these things in your vision, how would you describe them? It appears John saw aircraft and helicopters. The sounds of wings. The sounds of jet airplanes and propellers sound like many horsemen and chariots going to battle. If you do some research on the helicopters and planes, then soldiers painted faces on a lot of them. It's possible John saw some of these things in his vision. Something else about this prophecy that's very important we can't miss. Have the sun and moon ever been darkened by smoke before? As far as I know, they haven't been, and not for several months at a time. *Revelation 9:11* identifies the key holder of *(Revelation 9:1)* as a King and gives

43

The Endtime Is Now

specific, identifiable terms for him. The dictionary defines both Abaddon in Hebrew and Apollyon in Greek as "The Destroyer." The name Saddam means "Crusher" or "Destroyer." Saddam "The Destroyer" Hussein. The "key holder," Saddam, ordered those oil wells to be set on fire.

Verses 5 and 6 almost describe a scare campaign, during the Gulf War, when they saw U.S. troops coming, they surrendered immediately, instead of fighting back. This went on for months. There are a couple of small parts of this prophecy I'm not able to explain or identify as clearly as I would like. It's like proving that in World War II, one-third of the sea creatures were killed during that time. Sometimes you may not be able to provide evidence for certain things. However, with most of the information identified here, one can conclude that this is the understanding of the 5th Trumpet.

The 6th Trumpet (2nd Woe)

> 13 Then the **sixth angel sounded**: And I heard a voice from the four horns of the golden altar which is before God, 14 saying to the sixth angel who had the trumpet, **"Release the four angels who are bound at the great river Euphrates."** 15 So the four angels, who had been prepared for the hour and day and month and year, **were released to kill a third of mankind**. 16 Now the number of the army of the horsemen was **two hundred million**; I heard the number of them. Revelation 9:13-16 NKJV

The 6th Trumpet War kills 1/3 of mankind and will start from the Euphrates River area, and an army of 200 million men will participate in this war. No war like this has happened so far. Every nuclear superpower today has ties to the Middle East, with the United States and Russia both being the largest nuclear powers. They both currently operate positions on opposite sides of the Euphrates River today. There are about 8 billion people on earth today, 1/3 of them would be around 2.6 billion people. 8.2 million were killed in WW1, 52 million were killed in WW2, and 2.6 billion will be killed in the 6th trumpet war. That's 50 times the number of deaths of World War II.

This war starts in the area of the Euphrates River. Four nations house this river: Syria, Iraq, Iran, and Turkey. Who will make up the 200 million-man army? A few powers with a large enough population could do that today: China, India, and Islam. One other idea is that the 200 million-man army could be suggesting the total combined fighters from all involved. A coalition army. Islam will be a part of this war because the war begins from the Euphrates, a 100% Islamic river. The angels are represented as evil spirits. Godly angels are not bound. These angels are most likely representative of the spirits of these four nations that house the Euphrates River. As we have learned from the 4th Seal, the Pale Green Horse, death follows.

> *17 And thus I saw the horses in the vision: those who sat on them had breastplates of fiery red, hyacinth blue, and sulfur yellow; and the heads of the horses were like the heads of lions; and out of their mouths came fire, smoke, and brimstone. 18 By these three plagues **a third of mankind was killed—by the fire and the smoke and the brimstone** which came out of their mouths. 19 For their power is in their mouth and in their tails; for their tails are like serpents, having heads; and with them they do harm. Revelation 9:17-19 NKJV*

This is 1/3 of all humans on earth being killed with what John appears to be describing as the destruction by nuclear warfare (fire, smoke, brimstone), 1/3 are killed by these three.

> *20 But the rest of mankind, who were not killed by these plagues, did not repent of the works of their hands, that they should not worship demons, and idols of gold, silver, brass, stone, and wood, which can neither see nor hear nor walk. 21 And they did not repent of their murders or their sorceries or their sexual immorality or their thefts. Revelation 9:20-21 NKJV*

First, we know that up to this point, the Antichrist has not yet been publicly revealed. We know this because the people still do not repent after this horrific war. They are rebuked for worshiping everything but the Antichrist; they are going to turn to human answers and his one-world government. The League of Nations was established after World War I, and the United Nations after World War II, both with the intention of preventing future world wars. After this war, I'm sure it will usher in a full-blown global government led by the Antichrist.

One may be wondering when the timing of this great war is. Chapters 10 and 11 of Revelation record events that follow the sixth Trumpet war but precede the seventh Trumpet. Chapter 11 records the ministry of the two witnesses. These two witnesses do not appear on the scene until the Abomination of Desolation takes place. Their ministry is exactly 1260 days or 3 1/2 years, the same as the Antichrist's reign. We already know that the Abomination of Desolation doesn't occur until the midpoint of the seven-year period. So, in conclusion, we can confidently say that this war will be before the Abomination of Desolation, most likely after the peace agreement of Daniel 9:27, the confirmation of the covenant. This war will take place during the first half of the seven-year period or just prior to the peace agreement, not during the second half, which will be the Great Tribulation. Interestingly, many Bible scholars suggest that the Ezekiel 38-39 war of Gog and Magog will happen just before or at the beginning of the final seven years. I do believe the 6th Trumpet war and the Gog and Magog war are the same. Ezekiel gives more details of all the participants of the war geopolitically, whereas Revelation 9 provides details of the destruction; both overlap with some of the same participants that include the four spirits or countries that house the Euphrates River: Syria, Turkey, Iraq, and Iran. So a coalition army of many nations will likely be the makeup of the 200 million-man army that's mentioned in Revelation 9. One may be asking, where is the United States during this war? We learned in principle 3 that the Eagle's Wings of the United States are protecting Israel for 3 1/2 years from the presence of Satan during the Great Tribulation (Revelation 12:14), and we learned from principle 1 that the Great Tribulation doesn't begin until the second half of the seven years. So, from this understanding, it appears the U.S. survives this 6th Trumpet war but not without judgment from God. As we look at Ezekiel 39:6, the most secure nation on the planet during this war is found to have what appears to be a nuclear exchange with Russia.

> 6"And I will send **fire** on **Magog** and on **those who live in security in the coastlands**. Then they shall know that I am the Lord. Ezekiel 39:6

It goes without question that the United States is the most secure nation on this planet today, with the strongest military in modern history, not to mention that the United States is surrounded mostly by coastlines east, west, and south, not to mention Hawaii, which is completely surrounded. It appears the U.S. is inserted into this war due to Russia (Magog) and its other allies' aggressive attack against Israel. This may also suggest that most U.S. casualties from this war will be in coastal areas. After this war, as I stated earlier, most of the world will turn to human answers for solutions; however, there will be some who will *"know that I am the Lord."* I believe the United States will be among the latter group, hence the reason we see the Eagle's Wings protection of Israel during the 3 1/2 year Great Tribulation that will follow shortly afterward when the Abomination of Desolation occurs, spoken of by Daniel 9:27.

I've created a comparison table of the Revelation 9 sixth trumpet war to the Ezekiel 38-39 Gog & Magog war. If both wars do in fact happen before the abomination of desolation, as have been described they are. In that case, it goes without doubt how these nations would be able to be involved in both wars in such short proximity due to the massive destruction and death both cause, unless what is being described is actually the same war from two different accounts in the Bible.

WORLD WAR III

Two-Angle Comparison

6th TRUMPET WAR — REVELATION ch. 9 | GOG & MAGOG — EZEKIEL ch. 38-39

6th TRUMPET WAR — REVELATION ch. 9	GOG & MAGOG — EZEKIEL ch. 38-39
{A Massive Army} ⟷	**{A Massive Army}**
The location of the launch of WW3 will be from the Middle East and points to some of the same main participants of the Gog & Magog war against Israel	Here in Ezekiel, he repeatedly emphasizes the massive army that will be coming against Israel
Revelation 9:14 saying to the sixth angel who had the trumpet, "Release the **four angels** who are bound at the **great river Euphrates**." *(God's angels aren't bound; this appears to be referring to the angels of the only four countries that house the Euphrates River: Turkey, Syria, Iraq, and Iran.)*	**Ezekiel 38:4** Army, Great Company
	Ezekiel 38:6 Many people are with you
It can't get any clearer than this of the massive size of this coalition army	**Ezekiel 38:7** all your companies gathered about you
Revelation 9:16 Now the number of the army of the horsemen were **200 million**, I heard the number of them.	**Ezekiel 38:9** Coming like a storm covering the land like a cloud
	Ezekiel 38:9 you and all your troops and many peoples with you
I certainly could understand why a 200 million-man army might be described as a storm cloud by Ezekiel	**Ezekiel 38:13** gathered your army
	Ezekiel 38:15 Many peoples with you
	Ezekiel 38:15 a great company and mighty army
	Ezekiel 38:16 Like a cloud, to cover the land
	Ezekiel 38:22 on his troops, and on the many peoples who are with him
	Ezekiel 39:4 all your troops and the peoples who are with you
{Tools of Destruction} ⟷	**{Tools of Destruction}**
Revelation 9:18 Fire, Smoke, and Brimstone *(nuclear warfare)*	**Ezekiel 38:19** Fire, great earthquake in mountains of Israel
	Ezekiel 39:20 <u>Mountains</u> shall be <u>thrown down</u>, the steep places shall fall *(same terminology used during the 1st and 2nd Trumpets, WW1 & WW2) nuclear fallout*
	Ezekiel 39:22 I will <u>rain down</u> on him, on his troops, and on the many peoples who are with him, flooding rain, **great hailstones, fire, and brimstone.**
	Ezekiel 39:6 I will send Fire

The Endtime Is Now

{Massive Global Death}	{Massive Global Death}
Revelation 9:15 So the four angels, who had been prepared for the hour and day and month and year, were released to **kill a third of mankind.** *(Today that would equate to over 2.4 Billion people)*	**Ezekiel 39:6** "And I will send **fire** on **Magog** and on those who **live in security in the coastlands.** *(Indication that this war goes global: those who live in security in the coastlands aren't referring to Israel but however Israel's strongest ally, the U.S. This may be a nuclear fallout between Russia and the United States the most secure nation on the planet)*
Revelation 9:18 By these three plagues **a third of mankind was killed**—by the fire and the smoke and the brimstone which came out of their mouths.	**Ezekiel 39:11, 12** …they will bury Gog and his multitude…For 7 months the house of Israel will be burying them…*(In Israel alone, it will take them a long length of time to bury the dead, which indicates massive death.)*

{Timing of WAR}	{Timing of WAR}
The 6th Trumpet War is recorded in chapter 9. **Chapters 10 and 11 of Revelation are events recorded that follow after the sixth Trumpet war but before the 7th Trumpet.** Chapter 11 records the ministry of the two witnesses. These two witnesses do not appear on the scene until the Abomination of Desolation occurs. Their ministry is precisely 1260 days or 3 1/2 years, the same as the Antichrist's reign. The two witnesses die lying in the streets for 3 1/2 days before they are resurrected within the same hour of the 7th and final trumpet sounding, the rapture. We already know that the Abomination of Desolation doesn't occur until the midpoint of the seven-year period. **So, in conclusion, we can confidently say that this war will be before the Abomination of Desolation,** most likely after the peace agreement of **Daniel 9:27**, the confirmation of the covenant. **This war will take place during the first half of the seven-year period or just prior/after the peace agreement, not during the second half, which will be the Great Tribulation.**	**Ezekiel 38:11** You will say, 'I will go up against a land of unwalled villages; I will go to a **peaceful people, who dwell safely,** all of them dwelling without walls, and having neither bars nor gates' *(Israel is living at a high level of feeling safe and secure. Until this point, Israel, throughout our recent history, has been under constant threat of terrorism from every side. Some have placed the Gog & Magog War as part of the Battle of Armageddon. Peace will not be the environment for Israel at the end of the final seven years. The Bible states Antichrist will be warring with the Jews and Saints during the Great Tribulation, final 3 1/2 years. The only time for this type of environment of safety will be after the peace deal of Daniel 9:27 which happens at the beginning of the final seven years not at the end.)*
	Ezekiel 39:9 "Then **those who dwell in the cities of Israel** will go out and set on fire and burn the weapons, both the shields and bucklers, the bows and arrows, the javelins and spears; and they will make fires with them for **seven years.** *(This is another proof that this war happens at the beginning of the final seven years. There will be no need for them to conduct this activity when Jesus rules during the millennium.* **Jesus himself** *will instantly melt everything with a fervent heat at his second coming* **2nd Peter 3:10-13**)

Both Wars Happen During The Beginning Of The Final Seven-Years

For when they say, "Peace and safety!" then sudden destruction comes upon them, as labor pains upon a pregnant woman. And they shall not escape.
1st Thessalonians 5:3

The Endtime Is Now

The 7th Trumpet (3rd Woe)

> *15 Then the **seventh angel sounded**: And there were loud voices in heaven, saying, **"The kingdoms of this world have become the kingdoms of our Lord and of His Christ, and He shall reign forever and ever!"** Revelation 11:15 NKJV*
>
> *18 The nations were angry, and **Your wrath has come**,*
> *And the time of the dead, that they should be judged,*
> *And that You should **reward Your servants the prophets and the saints**, And those who fear Your name, small and great,*
> *And should destroy those who destroy the earth."*
> *Revelation 11:18 NKJV*

The events of the seventh Trumpet. The Kingdoms of this world shall become the kingdoms of our Lord, while at the same time, Jesus will be pouring out his wrath upon the nations at the battle of Armageddon. It also states that he will distribute rewards among the saints. During this time, we will be changed from mortal to immortal to be caught up in the air to receive our reward of eternal life. All of this happens at the time of the Battle of Armageddon. One may ask, I thought the rapture would come like in the days of Noah? Everyone is eating, drinking, and having a good time, etc...The passage being referred to is found in the Gospel of Matthew.

> *38 For as in the days before the flood, they were **eating and drinking, marrying and giving in marriage**, until the day that Noah entered the ark, 39 and did not know until the flood came and took them all away, so also will the coming of the Son of Man be Matthew 24:38-39*

Interestingly, a few verses prior here in Revelation 11 are exactly what Jesus describes from Matthew, found happening after the two witnesses **(prophets)** are killed. Let's look:

> *7 **When they finish their testimony**, the beast that ascends out of the bottomless pit will make war against them, overcome them, and kill them......9 Then those from the peoples, tribes, tongues, and **nations will see their dead bodies three-and-a-half days**, and not allow their dead bodies to be put into graves. 10 And **those who dwell on the earth will rejoice over them, make merry, and send gifts to one another**, because these **two prophets** tormented those who dwell on the earth. Revelation 11:7, 9-10*

The 7th Trumpet is referred to in another place in scripture (1st Corinthians 15:51-53). Paul talked about the last Trumpet.

> *51 Behold, I tell you a mystery: We shall not all sleep, but we shall all be changed— 52 in a moment, in the twinkling of an eye, **at the last trumpet**. For the trumpet will sound, and the dead will be raised incorruptible, and we shall be changed. 53 For this corruptible must put on incorruption, and this mortal must put on immortality. 1st Corinthians 15:51-53 NKJ*

Another account also mentions the 7th Trumpet.

> *16 For the Lord Himself will descend from heaven with a shout, with the voice of an archangel, and with **the trumpet of God**. And the **dead in Christ will rise first**. 17 Then **we who are alive and remain shall be caught up together with them in the clouds to meet the Lord in the air**. And thus we shall always be with the Lord. 1st Thessalonians 4:16-17 NKJV*

Trumpet of God (Last Trump). This is the 2nd coming of Jesus and the Rapture of the Church. Who will be raptured up?

> *11 But if **the Spirit of Him who raised Jesus from the dead** dwells in you, He who raised Christ from the dead **will also give life to your mortal bodies through His Spirit who dwells in you**. Romans 8:11 NKJV*

It's vital that we have a relationship with Jesus Christ, whose spirit lives inside us. The spirit that raised Jesus will raise us up at the time of the Rapture.

(Revelation 11:19) Concludes the 7th trumpet.

> *19 Then the temple of God was opened in heaven, and the ark of His covenant was seen in His temple. And there were **lightnings, noises, thunderings, an earthquake, and great hail**. Revelation 11:19 NKJV*

These are the same events that were spoken of in the 7th Seal and 7th Bowl because they are all the same thing. The 7 Seals are the long story, ending at Jesus' return and Armageddon. The 7 Trumpets are the shorter story, ending at Jesus' return and Armageddon. The 7 Bowls are the very short story, ending at Jesus' return and the Battle of Armageddon.

The sounding of the seventh Trumpet will be the most unique occasion out of all the trumpets in the Bible, influencing every person! At this last trumpet, Jesus will send his angels to rapture all Christians for their reward and pass his wrath on the world's inhabitants. This event will mark the end of human government and the establishment of the Kingdom of God on earth for the next thousand years.

Seals
1st——————————————————————————7th

Trumpets
1st———————————————————7th

Bowls
1st—————7th

The 7 Bowls (Vials)

I want to take a moment before getting into the Seven Bowls to point out the difference between Satan's wrath and the wrath of God during the Endtime. Most scholars and pastors teach a seven-year tribulation full of God's wrath, therefore implying that the Church's rapture has to be before these seven years of his wrath because Christians aren't appointed unto God's wrath. Although we as Christians aren't appointed to God's wrath, the mistake made by scholars and pastors is in the details and understanding of God's Word concerning this matter. Some coined the phrase, Why would God beat his bride before the wedding? God will not beat his bride, but instead will receive a spiritually beautiful bride who will endure till the end. The real truth here is that the "Great Tribulation" is not God's wrath; it's Satan's wrath. *(Revelation 13:7, Daniel 7:21, Daniel 7:25)*

> *7 It was **granted to him to make war with the saints** and to overcome them. And **authority was given him** over every tribe, tongue, and nation. Revelation 13:7 NKJV*
>
> *21"I was watching; and the same **horn was making war against the saints**, and prevailing against them…. Daniel 7:21 NKJV*
>
> *25 He shall speak pompous words against the Most High,*
> ***Shall persecute the saints of the Most High**,*
> *And shall intend to change times and law.*
> *Then **the saints shall be given into his hand***
> *For a time and times and half a time (3 1/2 years)….*
> *Daniel 7:25 NKJV*

There will be events coming very shortly on a massive Biblical scale that the Church will be seeking answers to, and a response by leaders of an "opinion" or "most logical explanation" will not suffice. The Bible does provide us with clear answers, and the leaders of these churches need to be prepared to offer sound doctrinal responses during these times. As a pastor, hanging your entire eschatology *(27% of the Bible)* on one or two Bible verses taken out of context is irresponsible. It does nothing in preparing the Church and leaves them to their own devices, to all kinds of misguided false teachings out there. Also, Church history is a good tool for some studies; however, God states that a complete understanding of last-day events wouldn't be understood until the time of the end, Daniel 12:9-10. That time is now. My prayer is that if you're a pastor reading this book, it will assist you in your studies through God's word on this matter.

> *15 Then the **seventh angel sounded**: And there were loud voices in heaven, saying, "The kingdoms of this world have become the kingdoms of our Lord and of His Christ, and He shall reign forever and ever!" 16 And the twenty-four elders who sat before God on their thrones fell on their faces and worshiped God, 17 saying: "We give You thanks, O Lord God Almighty, The One who is and who was and who is to come, Because You have taken Your great power and reigned. 18 The nations were angry, and **Your wrath has come,** And the time of the dead, that they should be judged, And that You should **reward Your servants the prophets and the saints**, And those who fear Your name, small and great, And should destroy those who destroy the earth." Revelation 11:15-18 NKJV*

Here, God's wrath is mentioned. The wrath of God is mentioned when the 7th Trumpet has sounded. It's when the vine of the earth is thrown into the winepress of his wrath.
God's wrath has been poured out several times throughout the Bible. However, there is a specific time that God's wrath will be poured out upon humanity in the near future.

It also needs to be stated that even though Christians may suffer persecution by Satan during the Antichrist's reign, we will not experience God's wrath from these Bowls. We, as Christians, are now marked by God for protection. The 144,000 will be marked for protection. God marks anyone who has given their life to Christ for His protection up until that point.

> *2 Then I saw another angel ascending from the east, having the seal of the living God. And he cried with a loud voice to the four angels to whom it was granted to harm the earth and the sea, 3 saying, "Do not harm the earth, the sea, or the trees till we have **sealed the servants of our God** on their foreheads." 4 And I heard the number of those who were sealed. **One hundred and forty-four thousand** of all the tribes of the children of Israel were sealed: Revelation 7:2-4 NKJV*

> *13 In Him you also trusted, after you heard the word of truth, the gospel of your salvation; in whom also, having believed, **you were sealed with the Holy Spirit** of promise, 14 who is the guarantee of our inheritance **until the redemption of the purchased possession**, to the praise of His glory. Ephesians 1:13-14 NKJV*

Both the 144,000 and we, as Christians today, are sealed with the same seal for the one and only day of redemption. Jesus's return for his bride, the Church.

> *9 After these things I looked, and behold, **a great multitude which no one could number**, of <u>all nations, tribes, peoples, and tongues</u>, standing before the throne and before the Lamb, clothed with white robes, with palm branches in their hands, 10 and crying out with a loud voice, saying, "Salvation belongs to*

> *our God who sits on the throne, and to the Lamb!"......13 Then one of the elders answered, saying to me, "Who are these arrayed in white robes, and where did they come from?"14 And I said to him, "Sir, you know." So he said to me, "**These are the ones who come out of the great tribulation**, and washed their robes and made them white in the blood of the Lamb. Revelation 7:9-10, 13-14 NKJV*

Take note here of the "Great Multitude". This is evidence of the Great Revival that is to come during these endtimes. The Antichrist will have pockets of resistance and trouble on his hands. We will cover in-depth some of his opposition in the section titled "The Antichrist". Who will God's wrath be poured out on? Will it be administered worldwide?

God's wrath comes when the Seven Bowls are administered.

These Bowls will be a targeted campaign against the Antichrist, False Prophet, and all who follow after the Antichrist. We, as Christians, will not suffer God's wrath.

> *9 **For God did not appoint us to wrath**, but to obtain salvation through our Lord Jesus Christ, 1Thessalonians 5:9 NKJV*

> *1 Then I saw another sign in heaven, great and marvelous: seven angels having the **seven last plagues**, for in them the **wrath of God** is complete. 2 And I saw something like a sea of glass mingled with fire, and **those who have the victory over the beast, over his image and over his mark and over the number of his name**, standing on the sea of glass, having harps of God Revelation 15:1-2 NKJV*

The Bowls are filled up with the "wrath of God." I want to point out that the "Great Tribulation" 3 1/2 year period is not the wrath of God; that's the wrath of Satan. See:

> *5 And he was given a mouth speaking great things and blasphemies, and **he was given authority to continue for forty-two months (3 1/2 years)**......7 It was granted to him to make war with the saints and to overcome them..... Revelation 13:5,7*

> *12 Therefore rejoice, O heavens, and you who dwell in them! Woe to the inhabitants of the earth and the sea! For **the devil has come down to you, having great wrath**, because he knows that he has **a short time**." Revelation 12:12 NKJV*

So we can understand from this that the Wrath of God will occur at the end of the Great Tribulation. During the Great Tribulation *(3 1/2 years, a short time)* will be the wrath of Satan, not God. God's wrath, the Bowls are poured out at the end of the Great Tribulation. Most of the wrath of God is poured out at the Battle of Armageddon.

> *7 Then one of the four living creatures gave to the seven angels **seven golden bowls full of the wrath of God** who lives forever and ever. 8 The temple was filled with smoke from the glory of God and from His power, and no one was able to enter the temple till the seven plagues of the seven angels were completed. Revelation 15:7-8 NKJV*

There will be a time when God's wrath will be poured out upon the earth. Most pastors today preach primarily on God's love; however, God is a just God and is a God of wrath in the most righteous manner.

The 1st Bowl
(Loathsome Sores)

> *1 Then I heard a loud voice from the temple saying to the seven angels, "Go and pour out the **bowls of the wrath of God** on the earth." 2 So the **first went and poured out his bowl** upon the earth, and a foul and loathsome sore came upon the men who had the **Mark of the Beast** and those who **worshiped his image**. Revelation 16:1-2 NKJV*

The first bowl will not be poured out until the Mark of the Beast is administered. This gives us a timeline of when these Bowls start. We know that the Antichrist is revealed globally at the Abomination of Desolation, which is at the 3 1/2 year point (midpoint) of the final seven-year period. The Antichrist's time of reign is mentioned in several places, one of which is Revelation 13:5, which I shared with you earlier. This states power was given unto him to continue 42 months (3 1/2 years), the length of the Great Tribulation. We know this to be true because *(Daniel 9:27)* states that the Abomination of Desolation doesn't start until the middle of the seven-year period, referred to by Daniel as a week (Principle 1). Therefore, only leaving 3 1/2 years or 42 months for the reign of the Antichrist and the Great Tribulation. Jesus himself also validates this.

> *15"Therefore **when you see the 'abomination of desolation**,' spoken of by Daniel the prophet, standing in the holy place" (whoever reads, let him understand)......21 For then there will be **great tribulation**, such as has not been since the beginning of the world until this time, no, nor ever shall be.*
> *Matthew 24:15, 21 NKJV*

> *27 Then he shall confirm a covenant with many for one week; But in the **middle of the week***
> *He shall bring an end to sacrifice and offering.*
> *And on the wing of abominations shall be one who makes desolate....Daniel 9:27 NKJV*

These 7 Bowls will not begin until sometime after the 3 1/2 year point of the seven-year period. Most likely towards the end of the Antichrist's granted 42-month reign, near the time of the Battle of Armageddon.

With all the hype now surrounding vaccines and speculation about how governments worldwide plan to utilize them technologically in the future as a means of vaccination identification. I find it interesting here in the first Bowl that those who have received the Mark of the Beast do break out in smelly, gruesome sores. I'm not a doctor, but I do know that when your body tries to eliminate toxins and poisons from your system, it sometimes does so through your skin in the form of rashes, sores, and other symptoms. I'm not saying any vaccine now is the Mark of the Beast by any means, due to the fact that the Antichrist hasn't begun his reign, as well as other factors. If the seven-year period started tomorrow, it would be at least 3 1/2 years minimum from there before the Mark of the Beast could be administered, most likely longer towards the latter part of the seven-year period at the end of the actual 7th year; what I do see, however, as a "possible" scenario in the future is a vaccine/numbering/pledge system due to how this 1st Bowl is described in such a targeted fashion with what appears to be a pharmaceutical/supernatural side effect. This hybrid of vaccinations and implantable microchips is happening in Bangladesh as we speak. This is part of the ID2020 initiative. In my book *"Antichrist Unmasked,"* I dedicate a whole chapter to the "Mark of the Beast."

Some information about the Mark of the Beast can be found in:

> *15 He was granted power to give breath to the image of the beast, that the image of the beast should both speak and cause as many as would not **worship the image of the beast** to be killed. 16 He causes all, both small and great, rich and poor, free and slave, to receive a **mark** on their **right hand** or on their **foreheads**, 17 and that **no one may buy** or **sell** except one who has the **mark** or the name of the beast, or the number of his name.*
> *18 Here is wisdom. Let him who has understanding calculate the number of the beast, for it is the number of a man: His **number is 666**. Revelation 13:15-18 NKJV*

The 2nd Bowl
(The sea turns to blood)

> *3 Then the second angel poured out his bowl **on the sea**, and **it became blood** as of a dead man; and **every living creature in the sea died**. Revelation 16:3 NKJV*

We need to get a clean perspective of this bowl. It doesn't state that all of the seas would be plagued with this bowl. We can look at the plagues that afflicted Egypt during the time of Israel's captivity and the great exodus to get a perspective on these bowls. Many of the plagues of Egypt correspond to the ones prophesied in these Bowls. The plagues of Egypt were almost exclusively localized to that nation. So, these Bowls will only be poured out on those who take the Mark of the Beast, as mentioned in Bowl 1 and the Antichrist's armies, along with the region of the world from which his operation is. I firmly believe this region is primarily the European region, the territory of the one-world government of the combo beast mentioned in Revelation chapter 13, which we briefly touched on in Principle 3.

We will continue to prove this "targeted campaign" scripturally as we proceed.

The 3rd Bowl
(The fresh waters are turned to blood)

> *4 Then the third angel poured out his **bowl on the rivers and springs of water**, and **they became blood**. 5 And I heard the angel of the waters saying:*
> *"You are righteous, O Lord,*
> *The One who is and who was and who is to be,*
> *Because You have judged these things.*
> ***6 For they have shed the blood of saints and prophets,***
> ***And You have given them blood to drink.***
> ***For it is their just due."** 7 And I heard another from the altar saying, "Even so, Lord God Almighty, **true and righteous are Your judgments."** Revelation 16:4-7 NKJV*

The 2nd and 3rd Bowls are related to the waters turning to blood.

The one question that still bothered me after the 2nd and 3rd Bowls was: If this is a targeted campaign, how could these Bowls not affect Christians who may live in the region of the Antichrist during this time? We all need water. Pay attention not to miss what verses 5-6 say. It identifies God's wrath with a specific group of people. The ones that have shed the blood of the saints and prophets. As I have mentioned earlier and in (Principle 3), it strongly appears that the European region will be the hub of the Antichrist and his one-world government. I'm bringing this to light because when this Mark of the Beast is first administered, those who do not take it will be put to death quickly.

> *4 And I saw thrones, and they sat on them, and judgment was committed to them. Then I saw **the souls of those who had been beheaded for their witness to Jesus** and for the word of God, who had not worshiped the beast or his image, **and had not received his mark on their foreheads or on their hands**. And they lived and reigned with Christ for a thousand years. Revelation 20:4 NKJV*

Tragically, there will be very few, if any, Christians left in this region of the world, as it will be at the Antichrist's easiest disposal. Undoubtedly, the purpose of the timing and targeted campaign of God's 7 Bowls of wrath which is implied in verses 5-6 of Revelation 16.

The 4th Bowl
(Men Scorched by Great Heat from the Sun)

> *8 Then the fourth angel poured out his **bowl on the sun**, and power was given to him to **scorch men with fire**. 9 And **men were scorched with great heat**, and they blasphemed the name of God who has power over these plagues; and they did not repent and give Him glory. Revelation 16:8-9 NKJV*

Some people argue that this refers to global warming. However, we know this is not the truth. Global warming is not real and doesn't appear to be warming at all. Global warming is a worldwide initiative aimed at redistributing wealth and expanding global governance. One example that this is a hoax is that on January 26, 2006, the Washington Post stated Al Gore "believes humanity may have only 10 years left to save the planet from turning into a total frying pan." Well, folks, we are several years beyond his prediction, and we are still here; nothing has changed in the slightest. These predictions and dates are constantly changing and are long-dated, so that when the time arrives, you will have forgotten. They can continue to buy time to convince people of this hoax, furthering the global agenda and increasing the size of the global government. There is much more evidence beyond this, but that is a story for another day. Let's look and see what scripture has to say about global weather conditions as we advance.

> *22 "**While the earth remains**,*
> *Seedtime and harvest,*
> *Cold and heat,*
> *Winter and summer,*
> *And day and night*
> ***Shall not cease**." Genesis 8:22 NKJV*

The main point is that God is in control of our environment, not man. These Bowls are from God himself, and he is righteous and fair to do so. Sadly, during this time, people continue to rebel against God rather than repent.

The 5th Bowl
(Darkness & Pain)

> *10 Then the fifth angel poured out his **bowl on the throne of the beast**, and **his kingdom became full of darkness**; and **they gnawed their tongues because of the pain.** 11 They blasphemed the God of heaven because of their pains and **their sores**, and did not repent of their deeds.*
> *Revelation 16:10-11 NKJV*

Again, this is a very specific, targeted bowl. It says that this bowl is poured out on the throne of the beast, and his kingdom succumbs to full darkness.

There have been reports of low-lying, very dense fog clouds that have caused day to turn to night before. These types of clouds extend from the ground to several miles into the air, filled with moisture. Could this bowl be something like this on a massive scale? Maybe. The high humidity in the dark air would most certainly be painful to those gruesome boils and sores on those who took the Mark of the Beast—just a thought.

We now know that kingdoms refer to nations, and we also know from Revelation, chapter 13, that there is a picture of a cohesive combination of nations from Europe that will be the power hub of the Antichrist, with complete control during this time. It's this kingdom that this bowl refers to, as well as his throne, which could be located within this kingdom or perhaps even on the Temple Mount area, where the Abomination of Desolation occurred. In any case, both the Antichrist throne and his kingdom will come under this bowl.

During Moses' time back in Egypt, they were plagued with darkness for three days. This type of thing has happened before, as when God targeted Egypt to soften Pharaoh's heart. God will do these types of things again, much as He did with Egypt, at the end of the Great Tribulation.

Let's pause to compare the plagues of Egypt to the Bowls of the Great Tribulation.

1st bowl is smelly sores to those who take the Mark of the Beast. In *(Exodus 9:8-10)*, God caused boils to break out in sores on people throughout the land of Egypt.

> *8 So the Lord said to Moses and Aaron, "Take for yourselves handfuls of ashes from a furnace, and let Moses scatter it toward the heavens in the sight of Pharaoh. 9 And it will become fine dust in all the land of Egypt, and **it will cause boils that break out in sores on man** and beast throughout all the land of Egypt." 10 Then they took ashes from the furnace and stood before Pharaoh, and Moses scattered them toward heaven. And **they caused boils that break out in sores on man** and beast. Exodus 9:8-10 NKJV*

2nd and 3rd Bowls concern the waters becoming blood; we can compare that to *(Exodus 7:17-18)*, the waters turned to blood, and fish died as well.

> *17* **Thus says the Lord:** *"By this you shall know that I am the Lord. Behold,* **I will strike the waters** *which are in the river with the rod that is in my hand, and* **they shall be turned to blood**. *18 And the fish that are in the river shall die, the river shall stink, and the Egyptians will loathe to drink the water of the river." Exodus 7:17-18 NKJV*

5th bowl is Darkness & Pain. In *(Exodus 10:21-22)*, darkness was so dark that it could even be felt. They, too, were afflicted with boils on their skin prior as this moist darkness caused them pain. This plague on Egypt lasted for 3 days

> *21Then the Lord said to Moses, "Stretch out your hand toward heaven,* **that there may be darkness over the land of Egypt, darkness which may even <u>be felt</u>."** *22 So Moses stretched out his hand toward heaven, and* **there was <u>thick darkness</u> in all the land of Egypt three days.** *Exodus 10:21-22 NKJV*

7th bowl mentions great hail. We see in *Exodus 9:18* that God sent down great hail during Moses's time in Egypt.

> *18 Behold, tomorrow about this time I will cause* **very heavy hail to rain dow***n, such as has not been in Egypt since its founding until now. Exodus 9:18 NKJV*

In comparison to the ten plagues sent upon Egypt from God, the only Bowls not mentioned are the 4th and 6th bowls. It's amazing to go through these seven bowls and see what we can learn. This helps give us a picture because the plagues of Egypt didn't affect the entire planet; many were isolated to a specific region. Ok, let's move on.

The 6th Bowl
(Euphrates River Dries up)

> *12 Then the sixth angel poured out his* **bowl on the great river Euphrates, and its water was dried up**, <u>so that the way of the kings from the east might be prepared</u>. *13 And I saw three unclean spirits like frogs coming out of the mouth of the dragon, out of the mouth of the beast, and out of the mouth of the false prophet. 14 For they are spirits of demons, performing signs, which go out to the kings of the earth and of the whole world, to gather them to the battle of that great day of God Almighty.* **15"Behold, I am coming as a thief. Blessed is he who watches, and keeps his garments, lest he walk naked and they see his shame."** *16And they gathered them together to the place called in Hebrew,* **Armageddon**. *Revelation 16:12:16*

The Euphrates River is one of the primary water sources of the Middle East. This river will be dried up for the invasion of Israel in preparation for the Battle of Armageddon.

Interestingly, the Atatürk Dam gives Turkey total control over the Euphrates River. Turkey once almost dried it up when in a dispute with Syria back in 2014. Turkey cut the dam off as a weapon against Syria. The Euphrates River was jokingly referred to as the Euphrates Creek. If not by God himself, this ability to dry the river up by Turkey will most likely be used for the invasion of Israel by the world governing armies at the Battle of Armageddon.

Ataturk Dam, Turkey

"The Kings of the east" mentioned here is important because there is a group of people *(preterists)* who believe the Battle of Armageddon had already happened back in 70AD when Jerusalem was destroyed then.

Who destroyed Jerusalem in 70AD? It was the Romans under General Titus. If you look at a map, Rome is west of Jerusalem, not east. In Revelation, the Euphrates River is dried up to make way for the kings of the east to come down. Two things to take away are:

1) The Euphrates River has never dried up in history.
2) When it is dried up, the Bible says it's to make way for the kings of the east, not Rome from the west.

> *"13 And I saw three unclean spirits like frogs coming out of the mouth of the dragon, out of the mouth of the beast, and out of the mouth of the false prophet" Revelation 16:13*

The spirits are given authority from Satan (dragon), and these spirits are speaking from the mouths of the Antichrist and the False Prophet (whoever the Pope is at the time).

Warning! There will be some very influential and articulate individuals who will point people in the wrong direction in the future. Their message will be so deceptive that the Bible states that, if possible, the very elect (Church) could fall for their false message. We are beginning to get there now. Just take a look at how the Church responded to the COVID-19 pandemic. Some churches closed their doors to never open again, while others were staging vaccination sites on their properties for the "Greater Good," buying right into the lie of the governments of the world selling the idea of a quick solution under duress, an experimental, failed shot *(pharmakeia)* that killed and harmed many. People who call themselves Christians need to know their Bible, so they're not deceived during the endtime as we advance!

Vs 15 Right before the Battle of Armageddon, Jesus gives a final warning to those watching that His second coming and the rapture of the Church are near. This verse is not misplaced, as some are boggled by. It's right where God intended it to be.

For those not watching, Jesus will come as a thief in the night. The Bible says in other places that those who are watching, He will not come by surprise. *(1st Thessalonians 5:4-6)*

> *4 But **you, brethren, are not in darkness, so that this Day should overtake you as a thief**. 5 You are all sons of light and sons of the day. **We are not of the night nor of darkness**. 6 Therefore let us not sleep, as others do, but **let us watch and be sober**. 1Thessalonians 5:4-6 NKJV*

Vs 16 of Revelation chapter 16: As the armies cross the Euphrates River at this point, God has gathered the nations together at Armageddon, which means "Hills of Megiddo." This is where the Battle of Armageddon will begin and will end in the city of Jerusalem.

The 7th Bowl
(The Great Earthquake)

> *17 Then the seventh angel poured out his bowl into the air, and a loud voice came out of the temple of heaven, from the throne, saying, **"It is done!"** 18 And there were noises and thunderings and lightnings; and there was **a great earthquake, such a mighty and great earthquake as had not occurred since men were on the earth**. 19 Now **the great city was divided into three parts**, and the cities of the nations fell. And great Babylon was remembered before God, to give her the cup of the wine of the fierceness of His wrath. 20 Then every island fled away, and the mountains were not found. 21 And great hail from heaven fell upon men, each hailstone about the weight of a talent. Men blasphemed God because of the plague of the hail, since that plague was exceedingly great. Revelation 16:17-21 NKJV*

Vs 17 The statement "It is done!" I find it to be very significant.

Jesus died on the cross; he uttered the words "It Is Finished," bowed his head, and gave up his spirit. This meant that the full cost of our sin, which Jesus came to accomplish by ultimately taking upon himself the cross, had been paid in full for anyone willing to believe and trust in Him as Lord and Savior. By doing so, you become a part of the Bride of Christ (the Church).

> *16 For God so loved the world that He gave His only begotten Son, that whoever believes in Him should not perish but have everlasting life. John 3:16 NKJV*

Interestingly, now we hear the phrase "It Is Done!" It's at this point that Jesus gathers unto himself the Bride of Christ (the Church), and the rapture happens.

By comparison, both the Death of Christ and His return for His Church are partakers of similar events.

"It is Finished" Death:

> *30 So when Jesus had received the sour wine, He said, "It is finished!" And bowing His head, He gave up His spirit. John 19:30 NKJV*

The events following Jesus's death on the cross can be found here:

> *51 Then, behold, **the veil of the temple was torn in two from top to bottom**; and **the earth quaked**, and the rocks were split, 52 and the graves were opened; and **many bodies of the saints who had fallen asleep were raised;** 53 and coming out of the graves after His resurrection, they went into the holy city **and appeared to many**. Matthew 27:51-53 NKJV*

What do we see that happens?

- ☆ The Curtain was torn in the Temple from top to bottom, which symbolizes that the way to God is no longer through religion, but a relationship with Jesus is available to all.

- ☆ Earthquakes

- ☆ The Dead were raised from their graves and seen by many.

"It is done!" Jesus' Return *(Revelation 16:17-21)*

- ☆ The Dead will be raised, seen by many.

> *16 For the Lord Himself will descend from heaven with a **shout,** with the voice of an archangel, and with the **trumpet** of God. And the **dead in Christ will rise first**. 17 Then we who are alive and remain shall be caught up together with them in the clouds to meet the Lord in the air. And thus we shall always be with the Lord. 1 Thessalonians 4:16-17 NKJV*

Are the dots starting to connect? This is amazing!

⭐Great Earthquakes *(Revelation 16:18)*

⭐*Vs.19* The Great City will be divided into three parts. Just like the curtain veil was torn, God divides the city of Rome into three parts to destroy it in the winepress. Rome is the home of the False Prophet (current Pope at the time) and his false one-world religion. Jesus, who is the TRUTH, utterly destroys the deception of false religion. We will cover this more in-depth in the chapter titled "The False Prophet".

The "It Is Finished" and "It is Done!" statements have a commonly shared significance: The Bride of Christ (the Church)!

Verse 18-21, *Verse 19* of Revelation says that the cities of all nations will fall. This will be a worldwide earthquake, an earthquake like no other. This global earthquake will begin at the Mount of Olives when Jesus' feet stand.

> *4 And **in that day His feet will stand on the Mount of Olives**,*
> *Which faces Jerusalem on the east.*
> *And **the Mount of Olives shall be split in two**,*
> *From east to west,*
> *Making a very large valley;*
> ***Half of the mountain shall move toward the north***
> ***And half of it toward the south**. Zechariah 14:4 NKJV*

God's wrath continues when Jesus conquers the nations that rise against Jerusalem at the Battle of Armageddon.

In conclusion, we see here in the 7th bowl: noises, thunderings, lightning, earthquakes, and hail. These are the same events of the 7th Seal and 7th Trumpet. I will repeat that's because they all three are describing the same event. The Seals are the long story, the Trumpets are the shorter story, and the Bowls are the very short story that all end at the same point. Jesus's Glorious Return for His Church! Also, victory at the Battle of Armageddon and finally to set up His kingdom that shall reign here on a refurbished heaven & earth, for the next 1,000 years.

This also concludes the study of (principle 4) the Seals, Trumpets, and Bowls. As I hope you can see now, we are not waiting for the end times; the Endtime is Now. Having a Biblical understanding of all four principles will help guide one in their study of endtimes or eschatology. Having these four principles well understood should provide for a much easier understanding when studying other parenthetical chapters or topics. I will be covering a couple of different topics, and one of them includes parenthetical chapters, so you can see how having a correct understanding of these principles does make a big difference.

The 7 Seals are the long story, ending at Jesus' return and Armageddon. The 7 Trumpets are the shorter story, ending at Jesus' return and Armageddon. The 7 Bowls are the very short story, ending at Jesus' return and the Battle of Armageddon.

SEALS

1 White
2 Red
3 Black
4 Green
5 Great Tribulation
7th

The 4 Horsemen of The Apocalypse Are Not One-Off Events. Their Spirits Gallop Louder As We Draw Closer to the Great Tribulation

TRUMPETS

1 WW1
2 WW2
6 WW3
7th

BOWLS

666 MARK OF THE BEAST
1
7th

RAPTURE

67

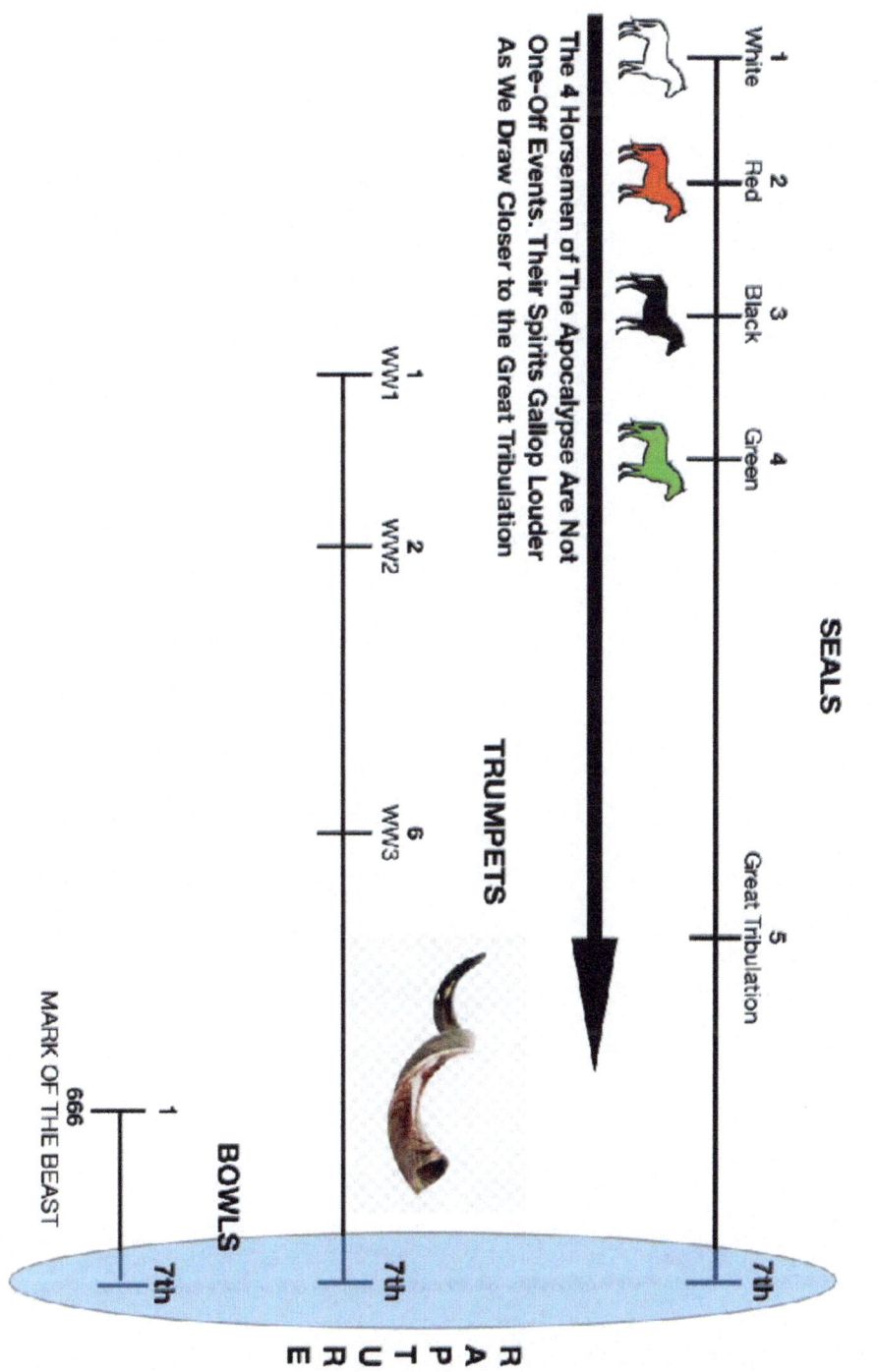

The Endtime Is Now

Prophetic Timeline

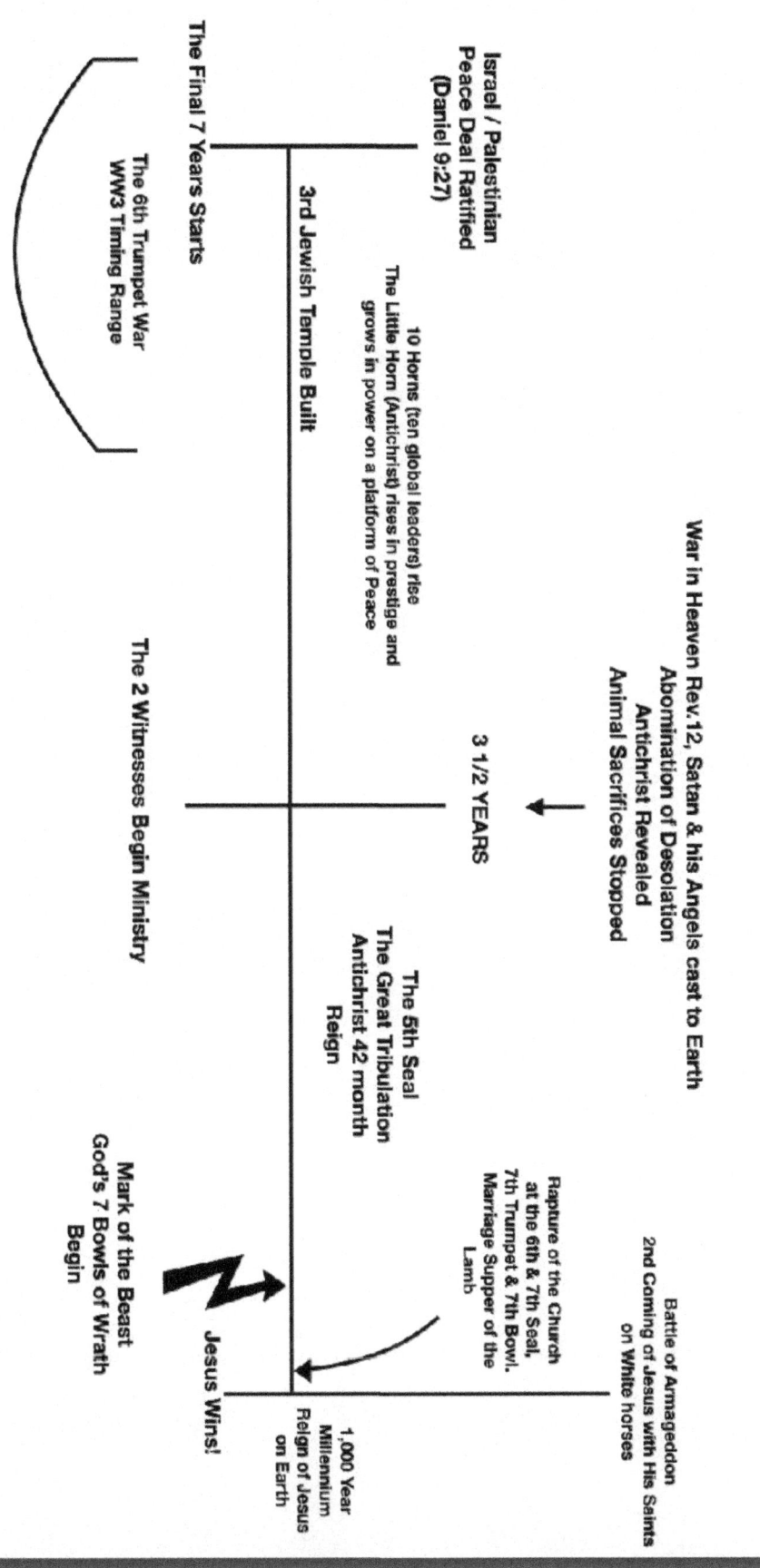

Israel / Palestinian Peace Deal Ratified (Daniel 9:27)

The Final 7 Years Starts

- The 6th Trumpet War WW3 Timing Range
- 3rd Jewish Temple Built
- 10 Horns (ten global leaders) rise. The Little Horn (Antichrist) rises in prestige and grows in power on a platform of Peace

War in Heaven Rev.12, Satan & his Angels cast to Earth
Abomination of Desolation
Antichrist Revealed
Animal Sacrifices Stopped

3 1/2 YEARS

The 2 Witnesses Begin Ministry

The 5th Seal
The Great Tribulation
Antichrist 42 month Reign

Mark of the Beast
God's 7 Bowls of Wrath Begin

Jesus Wins!

Rapture of the Church at the 6th & 7th Seal, 7th Trumpet & 7th Bowl. Marriage Supper of the Lamb

Battle of Armageddon
2nd Coming of Jesus with His Saints on White horses

1,000 Year Millennium Reign of Jesus on Earth

69

The Endtime Is Now

THE ANTICHRIST

The Holy Roman Empire has always been ruled by a political leader and a spiritual leader. The Bible prophecies that the Holy Roman Empire will be ruled again by a political leader and a spiritual leader. The political leader will be the Antichrist, and the spiritual leader will be the False Prophet. Satan himself will be the one giving these two their power and, by doing so, forming the unholy trinity (Satan, Antichrist, False Prophet). Let's start by looking at the Bible to see what's revealed about the Antichrist.

John identifies a specific person as the Antichrist while also teaching that there are many other Antichrists.

> *18 Little children, it is the last hour; and as you have heard that the **Antichrist is coming**, even now **many antichrists have come**, by which we know that it is the last hour.*
> *1 John 2:18 NKJV*

A Short list of Names given to the Antichrist:

2 Thessalonians 2:3-4 "Man of Sin" and "Son of Perdition"
2 Thessalonians 2:8   "that wicked"
Daniel 7:8   The "little horn"
1John 2:18   Antichrist
Revelation 13:4-5   the "Beast"
Daniel 9:26.   The Prince who is to come
Daniel 8:23   King of fierce countenance

Antichrist - One who denies or opposes Christ. One who puts himself in the place of Christ.

Where will the Antichrist come from?

> *8 I was considering the horns, and there was another horn, a little one, coming up among them, before whom three of the first horns were plucked out by the roots. And there, in this horn, were eyes like the eyes of a man, and a mouth speaking pompous words. Daniel 7:8 NKJV*

The Antichrist will arise out of a ten-kingdom alliance. We know from (Principle 3) that these horns represent kings or kingdoms. We know that these ten kings are the same ten kings represented by Daniel chapter 2 of the ten toes, representing the last of the five kingdoms on earth that would rule the world from about 600BC to the 2nd coming of Jesus. Here is a list of the last five kingdoms found in *Daniel 2:32-33.*

> *32 This image's* **head was of fine gold**, *its* **chest and arms of silver**, *its* **belly and thighs of bronze**, *33its* **legs of iron**, *its* **feet partly of iron and partly of clay**. *Daniel 2:32-33 NKJV*

The kingdom of the head of gold was the Babylonian kingdom; it no longer exists. The chest and arms of silver were the kingdoms of the Medes and Persians; they no longer exist. The belly and thighs of bronze were the Grecian empires; it no longer exist. The legs of iron were the old Roman Empire (197BC-284AD), and it no longer exists. *Daniel 2:33* describes a later kingdom whose iron mingles with clay to make the feet; this is the 5th and final kingdom that is rising today, the reborn Holy Roman Empire.

> *42 And as the* **toes of the feet were partly of iron and partly of clay**, *so the kingdom shall be partly strong and partly fragile. 43 As you saw iron mixed with ceramic clay, they will mingle with the seed of men; but they will not adhere to one another, just as iron does not mix with clay. 44* **And in the days of these kings** *the* **God of heaven will set up a kingdom** *which shall never be destroyed; and the kingdom shall not be left to other people; it shall break in pieces and consume all these kingdoms, and it shall stand forever. Daniel 2:42-44 NKJV*

This describes in the endtime, the 5th kingdom, with feet of iron combined with a new element, " clay," which symbolizes the reborn Holy Roman Empire. The Holy Roman Empire has always been from Europe. Pay attention to see that the ten toes are iron mingled with clay; this means the ten-horn Kingdom of *Daniel 7:8* will come from Europe, the Holy Roman Empire. This reborn Holy Roman Empire will consist of 2 leaders: the political leader Antichrist and the spiritual leader False Prophet. The Ruler of the Holy Roman Empire in every instance of history has always come from Europe. The Antichrist will come from Europe as its leader in the future.

The Holy Roman Empire was revived when the European Union was established and has continued to make steady strides in cohesion since the 2009 Treaty of Lisbon. Remember, the Pope and Vatican City reside within the parameters of Rome, Italy, as a theocracy with strong ties to the European Union today.

In the end, Jesus destroys this system to set up his Kingdom that lasts forever, referenced in Vs 44. Also, let me emphasize that Vs 44 also says that this happens in the days of these kings (Iron mingled with clay), not past kingdoms that no longer exist. This is another depiction of the transition of human government to Godly government ruled by Jesus that happens at his 2nd coming.

Finally, a last thought on this topic: Seminaries teach that Daniel chapter 7 with the four beasts is a mirror image of Daniel chapter 2. This is wrong, and you will be all messed up when trying to understand Bible prophecy concerning the enditimes. Daniel chapter 7 mirrors Revelation chapter 13, and instead of the kingdoms being described individually in nature like in Daniel chapter 7, they become a cohesive unit in Revelation chapter 13.

The Antichrist kingdom can be found in Revelation chapter 13.

Verses 1-8 refer to himself and his world government.

> *1 Then I stood on the sand of the sea. And I saw a beast rising up out of the sea, having seven heads and **ten horns**, and on his horns **ten crowns**, and on his heads a blasphemous name. 2 Now the beast which I saw was like a **leopard**, his feet were like the feet of a **bear**, and his mouth like the mouth of a **lion**. The dragon gave him his power, his throne, and great authority. 3 And I saw one of his heads as if it had been mortally wounded, and his deadly wound was healed. And all the world marveled and followed the beast. 4 So they worshiped the dragon who gave authority to the beast; and they worshiped the beast, saying, "Who is like the beast? Who is able to make war with him?" 5 And he was given a mouth speaking great things and blasphemies, and he was given authority to continue for forty-two months. 6 Then he opened his mouth in blasphemy against God, to blaspheme His name, His tabernacle, and those who dwell in heaven. 7 It was granted to him to make war with the saints and to overcome them. And authority was given him over every tribe, tongue, and nation. 8 All who dwell on the earth will worship him, whose names have not been written in the Book of Life of the Lamb slain from the foundation of the world. Revelation 13:1-8 NKJV*

The beast referred to here is about a kingdom and its leader. This beast described here describes the beast of *Daniel chapter 7* as now a cohesive combo beast, which will also include most of the nations on earth today. This coming together of nations represents the soon-to-be one world government led by the Antichrist himself. The nations represented here are the Leopard (Germany), the Bear (Russia), the Lion (Great Britain), and the ten-nation alliance (Holy Roman Empire). The Bible states in many passages that the Antichrist will rule this one-world system for 3 1/2 years.

For Example:

> 25 He shall speak pompous words against the Most High,
> Shall persecute the saints of the Most High,
> And shall intend to change times and law.
> Then the saints shall be given into his hand
> **For a time and times and half a time**. Daniel 7:25 NKJV

> 5 And he was given a mouth speaking great things and blasphemies, and **he was given authority to continue for forty-two months**. Revelation 13:5 NKJV

Verses 11-15 of Revelation chapter 13 deal with the False Prophet, the Antichrist's partner.

> 11 Then I saw **another beast** coming up out of the earth, and he had **two horns like a lamb** and **spoke like a dragon**. 12 And he exercises all the authority of the first beast in his presence, and **causes the earth and those who dwell in it to worship the first beast**, whose deadly wound was healed. 13 **He performs great signs, so that he even makes fire come down from heaven on the earth in the sight of men**. 14 And **he deceives** those who dwell on the earth by those signs which he was granted to do in the sight of the beast, **telling those who dwell on the earth to make an image to the beast** who was wounded by the sword and lived. 15 He was granted power to give breath to the image of the beast, that the image of the beast should both speak and cause as many as would not worship the image of the beast to be killed. Revelation 13:11-15 NKJV

Verses 16-18 mention the economic system utilizing the Mark of the Beast.

> 16 **He causes all, both small and great, rich and poor, free and slave, to receive a mark on their right hand or on their foreheads**, 17 and that **no one may buy or sell** except one who has the mark or the name of the beast, or the number of his name.
> 18 Here is wisdom. Let him who has understanding calculate the number of the beast, for it is the number of a man: **His number is 666**. Revelation 13:16-18 NKJV

Hmmm, during Covid, we couldn't buy or sell without a MA**S**K, and in some places, proof of vaccination was required; later, it will be a MA**R**K. The desensitizing, softening, and reprogramming are in progress. Now digital IDs are being created as a way to centralize everything about you, from banking, travel, welfare, and healthcare. Not to make life easier, but to ensure you comply with future edicts, or else be switched off. The UK is already implementing such a system to be able to hold a job. The United States has been coercing citizens to get on board with the "REAL ID," which is a national ID conversion mechanism to a Digital ID. The Lie to comply scare they are using is that you can't fly without it. That's totally false. They have been as ambiguous about the REAL ID as they were about the COVID shot. No one really knows anything about it other than the lie that you need it to fly. This measure of dishonesty and coercion that they keep using should raise red flags, but sadly, most are oblivious and couldn't care less right now. This is happening globally, and the dirty little secret that countries aren't telling their citizens is that the United Nations has spearheaded this new digital ID system. Soon, every national ID from all countries will be asked to convert them to a global ID—a piece of the puzzle in centralizing everyone's personal data and livelihood into a global database. No more passports needed!

It's one thing for your own nation to have all your information, but it's another when it's being tracked with power levers in the hands of a global entity. I'm a U.S. citizen and have no care at all about being a global citizen. This is where it's headed. We should push back at every instant when we can. Will it mean jumping through a couple more hoops to accomplish the same goal? Sure. Convenience is the lure to your future imprisonment. Right now, all but five states here in the U.S. will allow you to revert back to a traditional state ID. This will remove you from the digital system they are trying to implement here. They need to reach a certain percentage of the population to comply; we can reverse these numbers, throwing a monkey wrench in what they want to accomplish. At the time of the writing of this book, there are 15 other alternative IDs that TSA will accept, including passports, to fly. Guess what, if you don't have one of the 15 other alternative IDs, you're just asked to step into another line for "additional screening" where they give you a slip of paper with instructions on how to get the Real ID. It's all a lie, and you will be able to continue to fly.

The Mark of the Beast will be sold as an innovative, futuristic phenomenon of how we are to operate in society. Your livelihood and perhaps your physical life will be at stake if you do not opt into this global leader's system. God gave us free will, and Satan will be trying to take it away through this Mark. The system is being built faster than ever now, especially since AI came onto the scene out of nowhere. The good news they don't know is that God starts dismantling it as soon as the Mark of the Beast is implemented. Remember, the Mark of the Beast triggers God's 7 Bowl Judgements. The ten plagues of

Egypt have been estimated to have taken approximately 30 days to complete. These Bowl Judgements will not last that long, and we as Christians will be protected throughout them as the Jews were during the ten plagues. Afterward, they left. At the seventh and final Bowl, we go!

The Antichrist is on the earth right now.

Some speculate that the Antichrist is a system and not a man. This can not be true. Let's look at what the Bible says.

> *24 The ten horns are ten kings*
> *Who shall arise from this kingdom.*
> *And another shall rise after them;*
> *He shall be different from the first ones,*
> *And shall subdue three kings.*
> *25 He shall speak pompous words against the Most High,*
> *Shall persecute the saints of the Most High,*
> *And shall intend to change times and law.*
> *Then the saints shall be given into his hand*
> *For a time and times and half a time. Daniel 7:24-25 NKJV*

This passage references the Antichrist as a male figure, "He," not "It," but it also refers to the Antichrist as a king; so he would have to be a human male ruler.

> *3 Let no one deceive you by any means; for that Day will not come unless the falling away comes first, and the man of sin is revealed, the son of perdition, 4 who opposes and exalts himself above all that is called God or that is worshiped, so that he sits as God in the temple of God, showing himself that he is God. 2nd Thessalonians 2:3-4 NKJV*

This passage states that this will be a man who sits in the Temple, claiming to be God. This is also the description of the Abomination of Desolation described by Daniel and Jesus in Matthew chapter 24.

I hope now no one is confused about whether the Antichrist is an actual person, and that these few scriptures of many, along with the long list of attributes provided later, clear up any doubts.

The Antichrist will confirm a covenant

> *27 Then he shall **confirm a covenant** with **many** for **one week**;*
> *But in the middle of the week*
> *He shall bring an end to sacrifice and offering.*
> *And on the wing of abominations shall be one who makes desolate,*
> *Even until the consummation, which is determined,*
> *Is poured out on the desolate." Daniel 9:27 NKJV*

This covenant that is being referred to here is found in *Genesis 15:18*.

> *18 On the same day the **Lord made a covenant with Abram**, saying: "**To your descendants I have given this land**, from the river of Egypt to the great river, the River Euphrates. Genesis 15:18 NKJV*

Here, God made a covenant with Abraham, stating that this land would be his and his descendants' forever. The covenant that the Antichrist confirms will, in essence, agree on Israel's right to exist. The word "confirm" means to make better or stronger, so something else would have to exist to strengthen it. It also means to "Ratify," which is a vote to make legally binding. The "many" would be our modern-day United Nations that represents the many nations presently. Trump's Deal of the Century has already been announced. Israel, along with most Middle Eastern countries, is on board with it; however, as expected, the Palestinians are at odds.

At the time of the original publication of this book five years ago, the United Arab of Emirates signed an exclusive peace deal with Israel. They were one of the countries on board with the original Trump Deal. This made them the third country to make peace with Israel since they were declared a nation in 1948. Interestingly, they named this the "Abrahamic Accord". When this happened, the Palestinian Leadership's reaction was to be expected, not good. August 13th 2020, they tweeted, *"Please don't do us a favor. We are nobody's fig leaf!"* I found this comment very revealing and prophetic; keep in mind, they do not read the Bible.

> *32"Now learn this parable from the fig tree: When its branch has already become tender and **puts forth leaves**, you know that summer is near. 33 So you also, when you see all these things, know that it is near—at the doors! Matthew 24:32-33 NKJV*

There have been many commentaries that try to explain the parable Jesus gives. Most agree that the fig tree represents Israel; however, when it comes to the leaves, they say those must represent the events and signs prior to this passage as a lead-up to Jesus' return. I believe we just received a definitive answer to this parable on August 13th, 2020. Let me explain: the Palestinians implied in their tweet that anyone who acknowledges Israel's existence is a "fig leaf." As of August 13th, 2020, Jordan, Egypt, and the UAE were the only three that had made peace deals with Israel. They represent three fig leaves. If the fig tree represents Israel, then the leaves would have to represent those associated with Israel. For example, consider the "Lion with Eagle's Wings" or the "Leopard with Fowl Wings" mentioned in Daniel chapter 7 (Principle 3). Furthermore, Mark's account of the parable of the fig tree found in chapter 13:28-29 is the same as Matthew's account; interestingly, Luke's account is slightly different. Let's look:

> *29 Then He spoke to them a parable:* **"Look at the fig tree, and all the trees.** *30 When they are already budding, you see and know for yourselves that summer is now near. 31 So you also, when you see these things happening, know that the kingdom of God is near.* Luke 21:29-31

We find from Luke's account that the leaves have been changed to "all the trees". If the fig "tree" represents Israel, which is a "country," then Luke's account is suggesting that "all the trees" are countries as well. The leaves spoken of by Matthew and Mark are associated with the fig tree as other countries.

As we continue to see more and more countries making peace deals with Israel, this represents the leaves mentioned here in Matthew 24. Yes, this is a clear sign that Jesus' return is very near, even at the doorstep! Also, I would like to remind you what God told Daniel in *(Daniel 12:8-9),* that no one would understand his prophecies until the time of the end. We are being given clues now to understand these Bible prophecies; you just have to pay attention and know your Bible.

Now we are in 2025, and three countries have joined the Abraham Accords: the United Arab Emirates, Bahrain, and Morocco. If you include Jordan and Egypt, this brings the total of countries that have normalized with Israel to five. More countries are expected to join the Abraham Accords very soon. This will put tremendous pressure on the Palestinians and the global community that backs them to create a peace deal with Israel. When this happens and the day it's "confirmed" (ratified) with the "many" (U.N.) mark it on your calendars because we have just entered into Daniel's 70th Week, the final seven years.

Israel's persistent endeavor to reach a peace deal with what appears to be the strongest U.S. backing in recent times has brought about more discussions. Now everyone is at the negotiating table, including the Palestinians, and the pressure is mounting. Could the Trump Peace Deal be the one that is ratified or strengthened? It appears to be happening now. A little more time will tell.

One thing I would like to point out is that Daniel states this covenant will be confirmed with "many" for a week

(7-Year Period); the reason I mention this is that when a peace deal is signed between Israel and the Palestinians, as stated previously, it will also include many other nations. We know that the Antichrist will be among them, but it doesn't necessarily mean he will be at the forefront; he may be a background figure taking credit along with many other national leaders when this deal is announced and signed. Daniel does state that we will know for sure who he is at the midpoint when the Abomination of Desolation occurs. Also, I would like to point out that Daniel says this will be seven years. This may or may not be announced as a seven-year deal; the length of the time of this deal may just only last seven years. Everything may be agreed upon except the status of Jerusalem, which may be set aside to be revisited later, for I don't know, seven years. One thing is for sure: if you see a new Jewish Temple being built on the Temple Mount, we are, without a doubt, in the final seven-year period. You shouldn't be left with any confusion at this point, and I suggest you backdate the signing (U.N. Ratifying) of the Peace Deal and mark it on your calendars. Everything else going forward will be very precise as far as timelines during the final seven-year period. For instance, you can go ahead and mark your calendars 1260 days out (3 1/2 years) from the signing of the deal as when the abomination of desolation will happen and the start of the Great Tribulation. Also, this will mark the arrival of the two witnesses mentioned in Revelation, chapter 11. When announced, this covenant will be followed by a jam-packed seven years full of events (prophecies) culminating at the rapture and the 2nd coming of Jesus.

> *3 For when they say,* ***"Peace and safety!"*** *then sudden destruction comes upon them, as labor pains upon a pregnant woman. And they shall not escape. 1st Thessalonians 5:3*

This passage states that when "they" announce peace and safety, then certain destruction follows. I'm under the conviction that this "destruction" occurs during the first 3 1/2 years of the seven-year period after the signing of the peace deal. I can certainly see an upheaval when the Jews are finally able to worship in their new rebuilt temple on the Temple Mount that will also occur during these first 3 1/2 years. This passage could be referring to the 6th trumpet war that begins at the Great Euphrates River and kills one-third of mankind, World War 3—afterward, ushering in a world leader who puts a stop to the sacrifices and commits the Abomination of Desolation. At this point, the Great Tribulation would begin (midpoint) of the 7-year period. Furthermore, Daniel 8:25 says the Antichrist will use peace to destroy many.

> *25 And through his policy also he shall cause craft to prosper in his hand; and he shall magnify himself in his heart,* ***and by peace shall destroy many:*** *he shall also stand up against the Prince of princes; but he shall be broken without hand. Daniel 8:25 KJV*

My previous comment is of my own discernment and opinion. I want to be careful to make abundantly clear that the Bible doesn't state which comes first, the False Peace Deal or the 6th Trumpet War. I do know by looking at the Bible and current events that these two events are converging now at a rapid pace. All you hear now in the news is possible WW3 scenarios, at the same time, Peace & Safety is being touted. Really oxymoronic times we live in today. Either event could be followed by the other. The Bible doesn't specifically say which one of these prophecies comes first. One thing is for sure: we are seeing that the Bible is correct on both.

The Antichrist will have resistance and opposition.

Of course, it goes without question that Israel will not be a part of the Antichrist system since the Battle of Armageddon is against Israel, led by the Antichrist.

> 14 And to **the woman were given two wings of a great eagle**, that she might fly into the wilderness, into her place, where she is **nourished for a time, and times, and half a time, from the face of the serpent.** Revelation 12:14 KJV

This passage states that Israel will be given "wings of a great eagle," protecting her for 3 1/2 years from the face of the serpent (Antichrist). We have already spoken in (Principle 3) about who these wings belong to; it's the United States. There is a misunderstanding that the eagle's wings here are just symbolic of God's sovereign protection and nothing more. Scholars refer to the symbolic use of the eagle's wings in *Exodus 19:4* and *Isaiah 40:31* for their rationale. However, as we discussed in (Principle 3), *Daniel 7:17, 23,* Daniel explicitly describes who these beasts are; Daniel states they are Kings and kingdoms, and we see these beasts mentioned again in Revelation chapter 13 as a cohesive combo beast under the rule of the Antichrist. The Eagles' wings are nowhere to be found; that's because they are here earlier in chapter 12. Therefore, to compare *Revelation 12:14* to Exodus or Isaiah is an incorrect analysis based on the detailed information we received from Daniel about these symbols and their meanings during the endtime.

The country of Jordan will not be part of the Antichrist one-world system either. We know this from *Daniel 11:41*

> 41 He shall also enter the Glorious Land, and many countries shall be overthrown; but **these shall escape from his hand: Edom, Moab, and the prominent people of Ammon**. Daniel 11:41 NKJV

All these areas mentioned here are in the country of Jordan. Jordan will never come under the power of the Antichrist.

> *44 But **news from the east and the north shall trouble him**; therefore he shall go out with great fury to destroy and annihilate many. Daniel 11:44 NKJV*

Here we find, during the Great Tribulation, that the Antichrist runs into more opposition. He's troubled.

The 2 Witnesses will be adversaries of the Antichrist and cause him problems for the entire 3 1/2 year period.

> *3 And **I will give power to my two witnesses**, and **they will prophesy one thousand two hundred and sixty days**, clothed in sackcloth."4 These are the two olive trees and the two lampstands standing before the God of the earth. 5 **And if anyone wants to harm them, fire proceeds from their mouth and devours their enemies.** And if anyone wants to harm them, he must be killed in this manner. 6 **These have power** to shut heaven, so that no rain falls in the days of their prophecy; and **they have power** over waters to turn them to blood, and to strike the earth with all plagues, as often as they desire. Revelation 11:3-6 NKJV*

I'm telling you these things because the traditional belief is that the Antichrist will have complete control of the world without any opposition at all during the Great Tribulation. Yes, he will be a dominating force worldwide with much power and control; however, there will be pockets of resistance he will have to contend with. The discovery of these pockets of resistance in the Bible, which the Antichrist will have to contend with, also led me to question the meaning of *(Zechariah 14:2)*, which states that "all nations" will come against Israel at the Battle of Armageddon. This drew me to the conclusion that I explained to you in (Principle 3) that "all nations" referred to here have to be in reference to a world body that makes the decisions on behalf of all nations, which is now the "United Nations." This will undoubtedly be led by the Antichrist as well. The Good news is that the Antichrist and his partner, the False Prophet, both lose in the end.

> *20 Then **the beast was captured, and with him the false prophet** who worked signs in his presence, by which he deceived those who received the Mark of the Beast and those who worshiped his image. **These two were cast alive into the lake of fire burning with brimstone.** Revelation 19:20 NKJV*

Here are a vast number of additional characteristics and attributes that you can use to further your study of this person called the Antichrist.

Daniel 7:20 He will look more stout than his fellows
Daniel 8:23, the king of fierce countenance
Daniel 8:23 He will be a dark individual, very sinister
Daniel 7:24-25 He will be a man
Daniel 7:8 He will arise among 10 kings
Daniel 7:8 He will uproot 3 Kings
Daniel 9:26 He will be a Prince
Daniel 9:27 He will confirm a covenant that lasts 7 years
Revelation 13:1-2 His 10-nation alliance will converge into a union in which he will rule over.
Daniel 8:25 Will rise on a platform of peace and will destroy many by it
Revelation 13:11-12 He will be elevated by the false prophet
Revelation 17:3 He will be a communist or socialistic government leader (Red spirit)
Revelation 17:10-11 He will be preceded by 7 kings; he himself will be the 8th.
Isaiah 10:24 He will be of Assyrian descendant or have strong ties with ancient Assyria.
Daniel 7:8 having a mouth speaking great things
Daniel 8:25 He will cause deceit to prosper
Revelation 13:5 His dominance will last 42 months
Daniel 9:27 Abomination of desolation
2 Thessalonians 2;3-4 will claim to be God
2 Thessalonians 2:4 He opposes God
Daniel 11:36 He will speak blasphemies against God
2 Thessalonians 2:4 He exalts himself above God
2 Thessalonians 2:4 He will set in the Temple of God
2 Thessalonians 2:4 He claims to be God
Daniel 11:31 He will take away the sacrifices at the time of the Abomination of Desolation
Daniel 11:45 He will plant his tents of his palace between the seas and the glorious holy mountain
Revelation 13:7 He will make war with the saints
Daniel 7:21, 25 He will make war with the saints for 3 1/2 years
Matthew 24:15, 21 Great Tribulation started by the Antichrist
Daniel 7:7 He will rule a terrible, strong kingdom
Revelation 13:7 Power was given unto him over all kindreds, tongues and nations
Daniel 7:23 shall devour the whole earth.
Daniel 7:25 He will intend to change times and laws
Daniel 8:24 He shall prosper
Daniel 11:31 Arms shall stand on his part
Daniel 11:37 He will not regard the god of his fathers
Daniel 11:37 He will not regard the desire of women (No children)

Daniel 11:38 He will honor the god of fortresses.
Daniel 12:7 He will scatter the power of the holy people
Revelation 14:11 Mark of the Beast will be a mark of his name
Revelation 15:2 666 will be the number of his name
Revelation 13:8 all on earth will worship him except those here that are written in the Lamb's Book of Life
Revelation 13:18 The number of the beast is 666
Revelation 15:2 Antichrist will have an image
2 Thessalonians 2:9 Antichrist comes according to the works of Satan
Revelation 17:14 He will fight against Jesus at the Battle of Armageddon
Daniel 8:25 He will stand against the prince of princes
2 Thessalonians 2:8 The Lord will consume him with the spirit of his mouth
2 Thessalonians 2:8 The Lord will destroy him
Revelation 19:20 Antichrist is cast into the lake of fire
Revelation 20:10 Antichrist will be tormented day and night forever and ever

The Antichrist will fulfill all of these attributes listed and all prophecies about him. If he doesn't, he will not be the endtime Antichrist.

I believe the spirit of the Antichrist is alive and well today more than ever. I believe the person of the Antichrist is also present on this planet today. Things are moving at such a rapid pace. With every crisis, such as the Coronavirus (Undeniable Birth Pang), it appears the global government takes more significant leaps at controlling the masses and developing systems that remove more liberties, and that invade your privacy all under the guise of the "greater good." The global government system that has been underway for quite some time now, the Antichrist will soon usurp authority over it to accomplish his will. Based on all the attributes of the Antichrist, the Bible lists that I have studied more in-depth beyond what I have shared here. I believe I can identify him now and back it all up scripturally without contradiction, but I will refrain from disclosing at this time. There are several prophecies yet to be fulfilled concerning the Antichrist that will give us a positive ID as time continues to unfold; it only takes one attribute or prophecy not to align to disqualify a possible candidate. I hope this study will help you recognize him when he appears. I've written a book called "Antichrist Unmasked" that I would refer you to if you're interested in diving deeper into the Antichrist, which covers a lot of ground and provides a breakdown of the list above.

In closing, without a correct understanding of Principles 1,3, and 4, you would have been very limited in your knowledge of the Antichrist. As you can see, with a proper understanding, you can come away with far more accurate information about the Antichrist than any traditional belief. The Bible has clear answers for us.

THE FALSE PROPHET

*11Then I saw another beast coming up out of the earth, and he had two horns **like a lamb** and **spoke like a dragon**. 12And he exercises all the authority of the first beast in his presence, and **causes the earth and those who dwell in it to worship the first beast**, whose deadly wound was healed. 13**He performs great signs**, so that he even **makes fire come down from heaven on the earth in the sight of men**. Revelation 13:11-13*

The False Prophet will be the most famous and well-respected man on the planet. He will not call the Antichrist by the name Antichrist or any other titles that the Bible describes the Antichrist as. Instead, the False Prophet will exalt the Antichrist and persuade people to follow after him.

He will look like a lamb and speak like a dragon. He will look like a holy man, but his words come from Satan himself.

The False Prophet will be a highly influential and powerful figure. He will be able to perform miracles in a way that deceives people, one of which has such an impact that the Bible specifically lists it: *"he makes fire come down from heaven."* Just because a person can perform miracles doesn't mean he is a man of God. For example, remember in *(Exodus 7:10-11)* when Moses threw down his staff, and it became a snake. Pharaoh's sorcerers did the same thing. God does indeed perform miracles, and Satan is aware of this as well; this is why he will have both the False Prophet and Antichrist perform deceitful wonders to draw people unto himself.

So how can we be prepared? You need to know the Truth from False (lie). You need to know your Bible.

> *14 But you must continue in the things which you have learned and been assured of, knowing from whom you have learned them, 15 and that from childhood you have known the Holy Scriptures, which are able to make you wise for salvation through faith which is in Christ Jesus. 16 All Scripture is given by inspiration of God, and is profitable for doctrine, for reproof, for correction, for instruction in righteousness, 17 that the man of God may be complete, thoroughly equipped for every good work. 2 Timothy 3:14-17 NKJV*

So how do we understand that this portion of scripture in (Revelation 13:11-13) is referring to the False Prophet?

> *14 And **he deceives those who dwell on the earth by those signs** which he was **granted to do in the sight of the beast**, telling those who dwell on the earth to make an image to the beast who was wounded by the sword and lived. Revelation 13:14 NKJV*

This is a description of the False Prophet; we know this to be true because when we look at (Revelation 19:20), it matches perfectly. It's here that we discover his title as the False Prophet.

> *20 Then the beast was captured, and with him the **false prophet** who **worked signs in his presence**, by which **he deceived those who received the Mark of the Beast** and those who worshiped his image. These two were cast alive into the lake of fire burning with brimstone. Revelation 19:20 NKJV*

The False Prophet will also be the head Malefactor of the Great Tribulation.

> *15 **He was granted power to give breath to the image of the beast**, that the image of the beast should both speak and cause as many as would not worship the image of the beast to be killed. Revelation 13:15 NKJV*

> *16 **He causes all,** both small and great, rich and poor, free and slave, **to receive a mark on their right hand or on their foreheads**, 17 and that no one may buy or sell except one who has the mark or the name of the beast, or the number of his name. Revelation 13:16-17 NKJV*

Both the Antichrist and the False Prophet will demand that all follow the one-world government, pledge allegiance to the Antichrist, and the one-world religious system; if not, you will face death. The weapon that will be utilized to force all to comply so that they may participate in this economy will be the Mark of the Beast. We are closer to this type of system now than anyone may know.

Here is one example: As of 2017, over 90% of India's population is under an advanced digital system they have created, called Aadhaar ID and "India Stack," which utilizes biometrics, including fingerprints, retina scans, and face scans, to connect everything from welfare benefits to mobile phones. India's cash was forcibly reduced by 85%, and in turn, its people were forced to adopt its new digital system. It was the action of purposely reducing cash that forced those into this new digital system. There are other countries now experimenting with chip implants; for instance, Sweden is implanting its citizens with chip implants the size of a grain of rice in their hands to replace cash or credit cards. Here in the United States, over a dozen states are taking action and creating laws to ban the implantation of microchips. This is good for the U.S. and coincides with what we have discussed earlier, as the U.S. not being entirely a part of the Antichrist global system, and instead supporting Israel.

The United Nations has also been promoting the move towards a cashless global society. They have a goal to govern everyone on the planet by 2030. The ID 2020 summit will be held annually until 2030 with this objective in mind: to number every person on the planet. These efforts are in high gear as we speak, through a digital ID system spearheaded by the United Nations. The goal is for countries to develop their own digital IDs, which will later be easily converted into a global ID monitored by the UN. Whatever system is in place at the time will be what the Antichrist and False Prophet usurp authority over. The Antichrist and False Prophet will be "holding hands," so to speak, to force conformity into this socialistic system. The platform of the Antichrist is in high gear now and moving closer to completion every day.

> 13 And **I saw three unclean spirits like frogs** *coming out of the mouth of the* **dragon,** *out of the mouth of the* **beast**, *and out of the mouth of the* **false prophet**. *14 For* **they are spirits of demons, performing signs,** *which go out to the kings of the earth and of the whole world,* **to gather them to the battle of that great day of God Almighty.** *Revelation 16:13-14 NKJV*

The false prophet will be an enemy of Israel. Through their words, they will persuade the world's leaders to unite against Israel for the Battle of Armageddon. Antisemitism is already rising to dangerous levels; I can only imagine how severe it will become during this time. Since the False Prophet originates from Catholicism, it's important to note that the Vatican does not consider Israel or Jerusalem to be the holiest land, even though Jesus was born and walked there, and the Bible says God has written His name on Jerusalem. The Pope promotes Vatican City in Rome as the holiest place on earth. Perhaps this explains one of the reasons why the False Prophet would despise Israel.

I know we've already spoken about the Holy Roman Empire earlier; however, it's impossible to avoid this topic when addressing the False Prophet. Let's see if we can go a little deeper and nail this down even more.

The Holy Roman Empire has always had two leaders: a political leader from Europe and a spiritual leader from Rome. This tradition began in 800 AD, when Pope Leo III placed a crown on Charlemagne, also known as "Charles the Great," from Germany, declaring him Emperor of the Holy Roman Empire. The Pope has consistently served as the spiritual head of the Empire. Whoever is Pope when the Antichrist is revealed will be the False Prophet. While this statement may be offensive to some, it's worth noting that many Catholics also believe an evil Pope will eventually emerge. This idea originates with St. Malachy, an 11th-century archbishop who claimed to see a vision of 112 popes from his time up to the last Pope. Some interpret these prophecies to suggest the final Pope—or a Pope after the last traditional one—will be evil and that an earthquake will destroy Rome during his reign. These prophecies are detailed in the book "The Prophecies of St. Malachy.".

I'm not endorsing any of St. Malachy's teachings; instead, I'm simply explaining why some Catholics believe an evil Pope may emerge. Many scholars dismiss St. Malachy's visions as entirely fraudulent. As Christians, we know that true prophecy comes only from the Bible. Scripture alone provides the reliable source of truth regarding end-time prophecy—not false teachers, not celestial signs, but the Word of God alone guides us through these foretold events. I hope witnessing the fulfillment of God's prophetic Word will strengthen your faith as these events continue to unfold. This is one of my primary reasons for writing this book: to help faith leaders connect the dots so that they may equip the Church with solid Biblical answers. That the Church may be prepared for what lies ahead and for the greatest revival the world has ever seen.

Interestingly, the Bible teaches that Rome will be destroyed. It refers to this city as "Mystery Babylon" and describes it as the city of seven hills. Today, Rome is known as the city of seven hills. It seems I'll need to explain this further, so let's examine who "Mystery Babylon" is in the book of Revelation.

> *8 And another angel followed, saying,* **"Babylon is fallen, is fallen, that great city,** *because she has made all nations drink of the wine of the wrath of her fornication." Revelation 14:8 KJV*

When does the city of Mystery Babylon fall? This happens at the 7th Bowl. *(Revelation 16:19)*

> *19 And* **the great city was divided into three parts,** *and the cities of the nations fell: and* **great Babylon came in remembrance before God, to give unto her the cup of the wine of the fierceness of his wrath***. Revelation 16:19 KJV*

This is not to be confused with Jeremiah's prophecy of Babylon found in *(Jeremiah 50:1-40)*. Furthermore, in *(Jeremiah 50:39-40)* the Bible states this land would never be inhabited again, contrary to what some are teaching that this city would have to be somehow revived to fit Revelation's prophecy of Mystery Babylon. Nimrod built the original city of Babylon shortly after the flood. This city was built just over 50 miles south of today's Baghdad on the Euphrates River in Iraq. Jeremiah's prophecy of Babylon's destruction was fulfilled and hasn't been inhabited to this day. Saddam Hussein had intended to rebuild Babylon; however, his efforts were thwarted after the Gulf War in 1991. *"Let God be true and every man a liar" (Romans 3:4)*. Babylon, as described in Revelation, is called Mystery Babylon.

> *1 And there came one of the seven angels which had the seven vials, and talked with me, saying unto me, Come hither; I will shew unto thee* **the judgment of the great whore that sitteth upon many waters***:*
> *2 With whom the kings of the earth have committed fornication, and the inhabitants of the earth have been made drunk with the wine of her fornication. 3 So he carried me away in the spirit into the wilderness: and I saw a woman sit upon a scarlet coloured beast, full of names of blasphemy,* **having seven heads** *and ten horns.*
> *4 And* **the woman was arrayed in purple** *and* **scarlet colour,** *and decked with gold and precious stones and pearls, having a golden cup in her hand full of abominations and filthiness of her fornication:*
> *5 And upon her forehead was a name written, MYSTERY, BABYLON THE GREAT,* **THE MOTHER OF HARLOTS** *AND ABOMINATIONS OF THE EARTH. Revelation 17:1-5 KJV*

This "Mystery Babylon" is a different Babylon than what was spoken of by Jeremiah. Here in Revelation chapter 17, there are a few clues to the identity of Mystery Babylon.

⭐1) Notice that "Mystery Babylon" is referred to as a woman. If we go down to verse 18, we find that this woman is described as a great city, not a nation.

> *18 And the woman which thou sawest **is that great city**, which reigneth over the kings of the earth. Revelation 17:18 KJV*

⭐2) In *verse 1*, we find that this woman sits on many waters. *Verse 15* explains the meaning of these many waters.

> *15 And he saith unto me, **The waters which thou sawest**, where the whore sitteth, **are peoples, and multitudes, and nations, and tongues.** Revelation 17:15 KJV*

From the first two clues, we find that this woman is a city that serves as the power hub, presiding over a vast international system of nations.

⭐3) In v*erse 3,* we find that this woman rides on a beast with seven heads. *Verse 9* tells us who these seven heads are.

> *9 And here is the mind which hath wisdom. **The seven heads are seven mountains,** on which the woman sitteth. Revelation 17:9 KJV*

Okay, we now know that this city sits on seven mountains. Today, Rome is well known as the "City of Seven Hills." To be clear, these aren't small rolling hills that Rome sits on; they are mountains. Also, the Vatican claims to rule over 1.3 billion people worldwide as of 2018; we get this information from the census of the 2020 "Pontifical Yearbook." This makes the city of Rome an International power over "peoples, multitudes, nations, and tongues." Sorry to those who tried to apply this prophecy to the United States.

⭐4) **The woman is clothed in Purple and Scarlet** *(Revelation 17:4)*. The Catholic Church's two ruling bodies are the College of Cardinals and the College of Bishops & Archbishops. The Cardinals wear red, and the Bishops wear purple. Also, I would like to add that the woman here in *Revelation, chapter 17*, is also referred to as a whore. In scripture, God uses a woman as a symbol for the Church. For instance, Christ calls the Church his Bride. *(2 Corinthians 11:2)* refers to the true Church as a "chaste virgin to Christ." The use of a harlot by God was to describe a false Church of idolatry, etc. Just like what is being described here throughout Revelation *chapters 17-19*.

The bottom line, the Roman Catholic Church, more specifically the Vatican itself, is who the "Mystery Babylon" is. It will be this religious system that has deceived the people of the world and will continue to do so until the Battle of Armageddon. This is the religious system and its city of residence that will be utterly destroyed by Jesus at Armageddon.

> *19 And I saw the beast, and the kings of the earth, and their armies, gathered together to make war against him that sat on the horse, and against his army.*
> *20 And* **the beast was taken, and with him the false prophet** *that wrought miracles before him, with which he deceived them that had received the Mark of the Beast, and them that worshipped his image.* **These both were cast alive into a lake of fire burning with brimstone.** *Revelation 19:19-20 KJV*

Jesus will cast both the political leader, the "Antichrist," and the spiritual leader, the "False Prophet," into the lake of fire. Shortly following, Jesus will be crowned King of Kings and Lord of Lords.

We are living in some very prophetic times, and it will not be long; too many things are converging at the same time at a more rapid pace. We will know soon who exactly these two men are. As a Church, we need to prepare ourselves for an epic final battle against evil, and as the Bride, for the greatest revival the world has ever seen and Jesus' second coming.

Vatican City, Rome

THE GREAT REVIVAL & RAPTURE!

1 After this I looked, and, behold, a door was opened in heaven: and the first voice which I heard was as it were of a trumpet talking with me; which said, Come up hither, and I will shew thee things which must be hereafter. Revelation 4:1 KJV

Earlier in (Principle 2), I eluded to you that the Church is mentioned countless more times after Revelation chapter 4:1. The reason this is important is that I had been taught all my life that one of the main evidence that the rapture would be before the Great Tribulation is that you don't see the Church mentioned again anywhere after Revelation 4:1, and because the Church is not mentioned the Holy Spirit is also removed from the earth. I later came to realize that the reason for this belief is that the seven churches referenced in chapters 2 and 3 by John, after the last Church is spoken of, there is supposedly a symbolic rapture that took place in chapter 4:1, when John was immediately seen in heaven. They conclude this based on an "assumption" that this must be when the rapture takes place and the Holy Spirit is removed because John was seen in heaven prior to all the events taking place between chapters 4-22 that he foretells. They also try to support this idea of the removal of the Holy Spirit from the earth, along with the Church, before the tribulation, using (2 Thessalonians 2:7) out of context.

> *7 For the mystery of lawlessness is already at work; only He who now restrains will do so until He is taken out of the way. 2nd Thessalonians 2:7 NKJV*

So here they identify the one who restrains as the Holy Spirit or the Church. They interpret this verse as saying that until the Holy Spirit is removed from the earth, the Antichrist can't be revealed. Therefore, they are suggesting that because Christians have the Holy Spirit, the Church will also have to be removed (Raptured). They are implying a pre-tribulation Rapture. This all sounds great, unless you have identified "He" incorrectly, and the meaning of "restrain" is incorrect. Who is "He," and what is meant by restraining? To answer this question, we need to examine the passage in its full context, not just one verse.

*1 Now, brethren, **concerning the coming of our Lord Jesus Christ and our gathering together to Him**, we ask you, 2 not to be soon shaken in mind or troubled, either by spirit or by word or by letter, as if from us, as though the day of Christ had come. 3 Let no one deceive you by any means; **for that Day will not come unless** the falling away comes first, and **the man of sin is revealed**, the son of perdition, 4 who opposes and exalts himself above all that is called God or that is worshiped, so that **he sits as God in the temple of God, showing himself that he is God**. 5 Do you not remember that when I was still with you I told you these things? 6 And now **you know what is restraining**, that he may be revealed **in his own time**. 7 For the mystery of lawlessness is already at work; only He who now restrains will do so until He is taken out of the way. 8 **And then the lawless one will be revealed**, whom the Lord will consume with the breath of His mouth and destroy with the brightness of His coming.*
2nd Thessalonians 2:1-8 NKJV

From the beginning, in verse 1, we are told that this passage references the 2nd coming of Jesus and the rapture as one event. In verse 2, Apostle Paul is rebuking the doctrine of Imminence, not supporting it. This whole passage is a rebuke of the doctrine of imminence. In verse 3, we are told plainly that "this Day will not come unless the falling away comes first, and that the **man of sin is revealed**." You can't make it any more straightforward than this. Verse 4 here clearly parallels Daniel 9:27, the Abomination of Desolation, which we have already discussed. When did Daniel say this event was going to happen? In the middle of the seven years. The Antichrist can not be revealed at any other time; this passage confirms this. The Apostle Paul goes out of his way to make it clear what the revealing of the Antichrist will look like. So, just from this, we are already 3 1/2 years into the final seven years. If we look at verse 6, we are given the answer of who "He" is and the meaning of "restraining."

Answer: God and his timing. Many scholars see the phrase *"taken out of the way"* and automatically want to jump to the conclusion that this means the rapture. God wouldn't tell us one thing a few verses before that our gathering unto him wouldn't happen until after the Antichrist is revealed, and then reverse his answer a couple of verses later.

> *"God shall judge the righteous and the wicked,*
> *For there is a **time** there for every purpose and for every work."*
> *Ecclesiastes 3:17 NKJV*

(The entire Ch 3 of Ecclesiastes is devoted to Timing & God's Timing)

To add to that, Jesus couldn't come the first time until it was time for Him to come. See:

> **But when the fullness of time had come,** God sent forth His Son, born of a woman, born under the law Galatians 4:4

God controls time. He does everything in His own time; for example, your prayers are answered in His timing. This goes true for the Antichrist and his revealing. **The restrainer is God's timing for the revealing of the Antichris**t, not the Church; again, the answer is right there in verse 6. One last point: the Church is never referred to as a "He" but rather as the "Bride." After this event, we know that we have only a short time before Jesus' 2nd coming (Rapture) and the destruction of the Antichrist at the Battle of Armageddon, Vs 8.

Furthermore, we know that the Antichrist makes war against the saints (Revelation 13:7). During the great tribulation, we also see that Daniel states that God's people will be "strong and do exploits"(Daniel 11:32). In Revelation chapter 11, we see the two witnesses during the great tribulation with their ministry.

It doesn't surprise me now, knowing all of this, why the Church is so confused about endtime prophecy and the book of Revelation. There has been little incentive to truly understand the truth regarding this topic. After all, we won't be here, right? Was basically the entire book of Revelation written in vain, and for what purpose? Why would Revelation 1:3 state that those who read and hear would be blessed? How can the Holy Spirit be absent if the two witnesses are here conducting their ministry? These were some questions that I had.

> 19 Write the things which thou hast seen, and the things which are, and the things which shall be hereafter;
> Revelation 1:19 KJV

Revelation chapter 1 tells of three segments that John is to write about: the things which thou hast seen, the things which are, and the things which shall be hereafter. John was to simply write about the past, present, and future. Many have misinterpreted the 3rd segment. They say that segment 2, "which are" represents the seven Church ages and that the 7th Church is of the last age, and so when John ascends into heaven in chapter 4:1, this somehow represents the Church's rapture and removal of the Holy Spirit. There is no evidence whatsoever to support this thinking. John was given seven messages by God to deliver to those churches of his day. All of these messages can be preached in our churches today. John was following God's directive during his time. After John left the Isle of Patmos, he delivered these messages. These do not represent the seven Church ages. As we learned through the

Seals, Trumpets, and Bowls, the book of Revelation is not written in chronological order, and understanding the chronology of the book of Revelation is essential to comprehending the entire book. Scholars and some pastors have attempted to reconcile this idea, suggesting that because John was seen in heaven immediately after John 4:1, it proves a pre-tribulation rapture and implies that the Church is no longer mentioned beyond this point. This is not only false but can be easily refuted by the scriptures. Let's explore together where the Church is mentioned many more times after Revelation 4:1.

1.

> *4 And round about the throne were four and twenty seats: and upon the seats I saw **four and twenty elders** sitting, clothed in white raiment; and they had on their heads crowns of gold. Revelation 4:4 KJV*

The 24 elders represent the Church.

> *8 And when he had taken the book, the four beasts and **four and twenty elders** fell down before the Lamb, having every one of them harps, and golden vials full of odours, which are the **prayers of saints**.*
> *9 And they sung a new song, saying, Thou art worthy to take the book, and to open the seals thereof: for thou wast slain, and hast redeemed us to God by thy blood out of **every kindred, and tongue, and people, and nation**;*
> *10 And hast made us unto our God kings and priests: and **we shall reign on the earth**. Revelation 5:8-10 KJV*

The 24 elders represent every tongue, every kindred, and every nation, not just Jewish. *Vs 10* above states that the Church will reign with Jesus on the earth. *(Revelation 20:4-6)* confirms this.

> *4 And I saw thrones, and they sat upon them, and judgment was given unto them: and I saw the souls of them that were beheaded for the witness of Jesus, and for the word of God, and which had not worshipped the beast, neither his image, neither had received his mark upon their foreheads, or in their hands; and **they lived and reigned with Christ a thousand years**.*
> *5 But the rest of the dead lived not again until the thousand years were finished. <u>This is the first resurrection.</u>*
> *6 <u>Blessed and holy is he that hath part in the first resurrection:</u> on such the second death hath no power, but they shall be priests of God and of Christ, and shall reign with him a thousand years. Revelation 20:4-6 KJV*

"They lived and reigned with Christ a 1,000 years". This is the first resurrection. There are not many resurrections; there is only one first resurrection. The Rapture!

> *21 I beheld, and the same horn made war with the **saints**, and prevailed against them; 22 Until the Ancient of days came (Jesus), and judgment was given to the **saints of the most High**; and the time came that the **saints possessed the kingdom**. Daniel 7:21-22 KJV*

If the saints are to possess the kingdom and the 24 elders will reign with Jesus, we can confidently say that the 24 elders represent the Church or the Saints of Jesus Christ. It's essential to understand that the 24 elders represent the 12 apostles, the leaders of the 12 tribes of Israel, and the individuals who were saved out of every kindred, tribe, nation, and tongue. This is symbolic of the mixed Jewish-Gentile Church, just as in the early Church age of the New Testament. During the end times, Jesus will return to receive a combined Jewish/Gentile Church.

> *13 And one of the elders answered, saying unto me, What are these which are arrayed in white robes? and whence came they? 14 And I said unto him, Sir, thou knowest. And he said to me, These are they which **came out of great tribulation**, and have washed their robes, and made them white in the blood of the Lamb. Revelation 7:13-14 KJV*

The main thing to understand here is that the 24 elders do not just represent the Jews but represent all of us, including those Christians who endure the Great Tribulation who have been redeemed and washed spotless by the blood of the Lamb, Jesus Christ.

2.

> *13 And one of the elders answered, saying unto me, What are these which are arrayed in white robes? **and whence came they?** Revelation 7:13 KJV*

When John was asked where they came from? The response given in *Vs14* was that they came out of the Great Tribulation. Who is "they"? It's the Church. Revelation chapter 7 is a picture of the endtime Jewish/Gentile Church. These people were not those who were raptured before the tribulation, but instead came out during the Great Tribulation, which indicates that the world's greatest rival is just ahead of us. We need to be preparing for this revival.

3.

> *3 And I will give power unto my **two witnesses**, and they shall prophesy a thousand two hundred and threescore days, clothed in sackcloth. Revelation 11:3 KJV*

This is a great place to conclude the account of these two witnesses we spoke of on page 44. If God is giving power to his two witnesses and they are prophesying, do you think they will be filled with the Holy Spirit? Will these two witnesses bear fruit?

> *11 And **after three days and an half** the **Spirit of life** from God entered into them, and they stood upon their feet; and great fear fell upon them which saw them.*
> *12 And they heard a great voice from heaven saying unto them, **Come up hither**. And **they ascended up to heaven in a cloud**; and **their enemies beheld them**.*
> *Revelation 11:11-12 KJV*

"Come up hither" is the same terminology directed towards John in Revelation 4:1. For John, it was to show him things that would be in the future. However, for these two witnesses, it was for them to ascend to heaven from the earth in a cloud, and their enemies beheld them. Remember, the Bible says the dead in Christ will rise first.

> *17 Then we which are alive and remain shall be **caught up together with them in the clouds**, to meet the Lord in the air: and so shall we ever be with the Lord. 1Thessalonians 4:17*

> *7 **Behold, he cometh with clouds; and every eye shall see him**, and they also which pierced him: and all kindreds of the earth shall wail because of him. Even so, Amen. Revelation 1:7*

Both of these passages state that we will meet Jesus in the clouds among witnesses. These two witnesses ascended to heaven, just like Jesus did. This is the time of the rapture. Also, if you look further down in Chapter 11, it states that in the **same hour,** the final 7th Trump sounds. The last trumpet! There can only be one last trumpet; otherwise, you impose contradictions in scripture that aren't even there. The 7th trumpet is the last trumpet. These two witnesses are a part of the Church. We sing hymns in Church today about Christ's return at the last Trumpet and don't even pay attention to what we are really singing about. Oh, how true it is, though!

Additionally, this suggests an actual, literal final hour. The reason I'm saying this is because there are scholars who want to imply that the final seven years are the final hour. Again, that idea doesn't hold water scripturally. The hour being referred to here in scripture is actually a literal final hour. We get a firm confirmation right here in Revelation 11.

> *13 In the **same hour** there was a great earthquake, and a tenth of the city fell……15 Then the **seventh angel sounded:** And there were loud voices in heaven, saying, **"The kingdoms of this world have become the kingdoms of our Lord and of His Christ, and He shall reign forever and ever!"** 16 And the twenty-four elders who sat before God on their thrones fell on their faces and worshiped God, 17 saying: "We give You thanks, O Lord God Almighty, The One who is and who was and who is to come, Because You have taken Your great power and reigned. 18 The nations were angry, and **Your wrath has come,** And the time of the dead, that they should be judged, And that **You should reward Your servants the prophets and the saints,** And those who fear Your name, small and great, **And should destroy those who destroy the earth."** Revelation 11:13,15-18 NKJV*

Here, we see that in the **same hour,** the two witnesses ascend into the clouds, the seventh and final trumpet sounds. The sounding of the seventh Trumpet will be the most unique occasion out of all the trumpets in the Bible, influencing every person! At this last trumpet, Jesus will send his angels to rapture all Christians for their reward (Matthew 24:31) and pass his wrath on the world's occupants. This event will mark the end of the human/Satanic government and the foundation of the Kingdom of God on earth for the following one thousand years.

When we see the two witnesses killed lying in the streets, we will know we are within 3 1/2 days of our redemption. When we see the two witnesses rise to their feet and ascend into heaven to meet the lord, we will know we are next to go within the same hour. So, no one knows the day or hour now, but we who are watching will soon know. It's an event timeline! There are no contradictions.

4.

The 7th Trumpet God rewards the Church. He didn't reward the Church back in Revelation 4:1.

> *15 And the seventh angel sounded; and there were great voices in heaven, saying, The kingdoms of this world are become the kingdoms of our Lord, and of his Christ; and he shall reign for ever and ever. 16 And the **four and twenty elders**, which sat before God on their seats, fell upon their faces, and worshipped God, 17 Saying, We give thee thanks, O Lord God Almighty, which art, and wast, and art to come; because thou hast taken to thee thy great power, and hast reigned. 18And the nations were angry, and thy wrath is come, and the time of the dead, that they should be judged, and that thou shouldest **give reward unto thy servants the prophets, and to the saints**, and them that fear thy name, small and great; and shouldest destroy them which destroy the earth. Revelation 11:15-17 KJV*

When Revelation is referring to the Saints, it's referring to the Church. Those who try to justify a pre-tribulation rapture will try to say there are rapture saints and tribulation saints. The problem is, the Bible doesn't say that. The Bible does not say anything anywhere about rapture saints, and then divides the bride into tribulation saints. There are only Saints. There is only the Church. Some pass before us that are dead in Christ that will rise first, and we who are alive will be caught up into the air. Other than that, there is no such thing as a pre-tribulation saint and then tribulation saints. There are only Saints and only the Church. This is the final 7th Trumpet account of the Church. God comes back to reward the Saints.

5.

> *7 And there was war in heaven: Michael and his angels fought against the dragon; and the dragon fought and his angels, 8 And prevailed not; neither was their place found any more in heaven. 9 And the great dragon was cast out, **that old serpent**, called the Devil, and **Satan, which deceiveth the whole world**: he was cast out into the earth, and his angels were cast out with him. Revelation 12:7-9 KJV*

The War in Heaven. Michael and his angels overcome Satan and his angels and are bound to the earth. Up until this time, Satan had been able to go back and forth. For example, Satan went to God in heaven to ask permission to tempt Job; this took place long after Adam & Eve in the garden. Pay attention to how Satan is referred to as "that serpent of old"; this refers to Satan in the Garden of Eden. It also refers to Satan as "the one who deceives the world" in both the present and past tense. Some believe that this war in heaven has already occurred. This is actually a future war in heaven that takes place at the time of the Abomination of Desolation. When Satan is cast down to earth, the person of the Antichrist during this time will be possessed by Satan himself.

> *12 Therefore rejoice, ye heavens, and ye that dwell in them. **Woe to the inhabiters of the earth** and of the sea! for the **devil** is come down unto you, **having great wrath**, because he **knoweth that he hath but a short time**. 13 And when the dragon saw that he was cast unto the earth, he persecuted the woman which brought forth the man child. 14 And to the woman were given two wings of a great eagle, that she might fly into the wilderness, into her place, where she is nourished for a time, and times, and half a time, from the face of the serpent. 15 And the serpent cast out of his mouth water as a flood after the woman, that he might cause her to be carried away of the flood. 16 And the earth helped the woman, and the earth opened her mouth, and swallowed up the flood which the dragon cast out of his mouth. 17 And **the dragon** was wroth*

> with the woman, and went to make war with the **remnant** of her seed, which keep the commandments of God, **and have the testimony of Jesus Christ**. Revelation 12:12-17 KJV

This is referring to the Great Tribulation, Satan's wrath. *Vs17* says Satan went to make war with the remnant of her seed that keeps God's commandments and has the testimony of Jesus Christ. This is the Church!

6.

> 7 And it was given unto him to make war with the **saints**, and to overcome them: and power was given him over all kindreds, and tongues, and nations. Revelation 13:7 KJV

Power will be given to the Antichrist to make war against the Saints (the Church). There is only one Church and only one bride, not two of either. The bride meets her bridegroom at his one and only appearing.

> 10 He that leadeth into captivity shall go into captivity: he that killeth with the sword must be killed with the sword. Here is the patience and the faith of the **saints**. Revelation 13:10 KJV

Here, the saints are mentioned again. Just about every chapter through 22 mentions the Church in some way, except for a couple.

7.

> 6 And I saw another **angel** fly in the midst of heaven, **having the everlasting gospel to preach unto them that dwell on the earth, and to— every nation, and kindred, and tongue, and people**,7 Saying with a loud voice, Fear God, and give glory to him; **for the hour of his judgment is come:** and worship him that made heaven, and earth, and the sea, and the fountains of waters.
> 8 And there followed another angel, saying, Babylon is fallen, is fallen, that great city, because she made all nations drink of the wine of the wrath of her fornication.
> **9 And the third angel followed them, saying with a loud voice, If any man worship the beast and his image, and receive his mark in his forehead, or in his hand,10 The same shall drink of the wine of the wrath of God**, which is poured out without mixture into the cup of his indignation; and he shall be tormented with fire and brimstone in the presence of the holy angels, and in the presence of the Lamb:
> 11 And the smoke of their torment ascendeth up for ever and ever: and they have no rest day nor night, who worship the beast and his image, and whosoever receiveth the mark of his name.12 **Here is the patience of the saints**: here are they that keep the commandments of God, **and the faith of Jesus**.

> *13 And I heard a voice from heaven saying unto me, Write, Blessed are the dead which die in the Lord from henceforth: Yea, saith the Spirit, that they may rest from their labours; and their works do follow them. Revelation 14:6-13 KJV*

Here we see the *"patience of the Saints"* again. This is talking about all the Saints that made it through the Great Tribulation and the Mark of the Beast period who did not conform. Who are the Saints? The Church! Again, someone can argue that there are rapture saints and tribulation saints. However, you can not find any scriptures to support that. Furthermore, almost all Bible scholars agree that Matthew 24:14 is the last prophecy that's fulfilled before the rapture of the Church. It states that the gospel will be preached unto all nations and then the end will come. Christians are commissioned to take part in this privilege. Pay attention to verses 6-7 of Revelation ch.14, that the completion of this final prophecy is fulfilled by the Angels of the Lord right before the Mark of the Beast is doled out and the 7 Bowls of God's wrath begin.

8.

> *14 And I looked, and behold a white cloud, and upon the cloud one sat like unto the Son of man, having on his head a golden crown, and in his hand a sharp sickle. 15 And another angel came out of the temple, crying with a loud voice to him that sat on the cloud, Thrust in thy sickle, and reap: for the time is come for thee to reap; for the **harvest of the earth** is ripe. 16 And he that sat on the cloud thrust in his sickle on the earth; and **the earth was reaped**. 17 And another angel came out of the temple which is in heaven, he also having a sharp sickle. 18 And another angel came out from the altar, which had power over fire; and cried with a loud cry to him that had the sharp sickle, saying, Thrust in thy sharp sickle, and gather the clusters of the **vine of the earth**; for her grapes are fully ripe. 19 And the angel thrust in his sickle into the earth, and gathered the **vine of the earth**, and cast it into the great winepress of the wrath of God. Revelation 14:14-19 KJV*

We covered this in (Principle 2) of Revelation's 3rd account of Jesus' 2nd coming. "The 2 Harvest". This passage parallels (*Matthew 13:30*).

> *30 Let both grow together until the harvest: and in the time of harvest I will say to the reapers, Gather ye together first the **tares**, and bind them in bundles to burn them: but gather the **wheat** into my barn. Matthew 13:30 KJV*

The Harvest of the earth is the wheat, and the vine of the earth is the same as the tares. In *Matthew 13:30*, the wheat is the children of God. The tares are cast into the lake of fire. *Revelation 14*, the Harvest of the earth is the wheat, and the vine of the earth is cast into the great winepress of God's wrath. The wheat in *Matthew chapter 13* is the Church, and the **Harvest of the earth** in *Revelation chapter 14* is the **Church.**

9.

> *15 Behold, I come as a thief. Blessed is **he that watcheth**, and keepeth his garments, lest he walk naked, and they see his shame." Revelation 16:15 KJV*

The "Watchers" are the Church. God only comes back as a thief for those not watching and not ready.

The question I've been challenged with is: The Bible says no one knows the day or hour when Jesus is coming back, so how do you reconcile your position of a post-tribulation rapture? First of all, I do not hold a traditional post-tribulation stance. Most post-tribbers still adhere to a seven-year tribulation, and I have found that this one principle being misunderstood has flawed the details and timelines of events they describe. However, the passage they are referring to when asking me this question is found in *(Matthew 24:36)*, when Jesus was speaking to his disciples on the Mount of Olives.

> *36"But of that **day and hour no one knows,** not even the angels of heaven, but My Father only. Matthew 24:36 NKJV*

Some argue that Jesus was only speaking to those in the first century, not to people in the present. Additionally, some would say that Jesus, being God, is all-knowing and would have had to know himself when answering this question; however, he stated only the Father. Jesus, while on earth, humbled himself as a man while also being God. Now, he is sitting at the right hand of the Father in his full glory, so I'm sure Jesus knows now when he is returning. However, let's see if we can answer this question more thoroughly with more than just one scripture.

In *Acts 1:6,* The Disciples give it another shot and ask Jesus again from a different angle.

> *6 Therefore, when they had come together, they asked Him, saying, "Lord, will You at this time restore the kingdom to Israel?" 7And He said to them, "It is not for you to know times or seasons which the Father has put in His own authority.*
> *Acts 1:6 NKJV*

So was Jesus just speaking to the disciples here? Does this mean we will not know the times or seasons, either? The answer is found in *Matthew 24:34.*

> 34 *Assuredly, I say to you, this generation will by no means pass away till all these things take place.* Matthew 24:34 NKJV

The generation being referred to here is the endtime generation. We are the generation that was given all the signs and warnings to watch for, for example, wars, rumors of wars, famines, pestilences, and even the Antichrist's rise to power. Paul, in *(1 Thessalonians 5:1-5)*, clearly tells us we will have an advantage on timelines as time draws nearer.

> 1 But concerning the **times and the seasons**, brethren, you have no need that I should write to you. 2 For **you yourselves know perfectly that the day of the Lord so comes as a thief** in the night. 3 For when they say, "Peace and safety!" then sudden destruction comes upon them, as labor pains upon a pregnant woman. And they shall not escape. **4 But you, brethren, are not in darkness, so that this Day should overtake you as a thief**. 5 **You are all sons of light** and sons of the day. We are not of the night nor of darkness. 1stThessalonians 5:1-5 NKJV

Alright, we are getting a lot closer to the answer here. This settles the dispute about the times and seasons. If we pay attention, we will see the day of the lord coming, unlike the first-century Church. Let's see what else Jesus has to say about this topic.

> 42 **Watch** therefore, for you do not know what hour your Lord is coming. 43 But know this, that **if the master of the house had known what hour the thief would come**, he would have **watched** and not allowed his house to be broken into. 44 Therefore you also **be ready**, for the Son of Man is coming at an hour you do not expect. Matthew 24:42-44 NKJV

The "thief" represents the lord here, and the "master" represents unbelievers. The master lives in darkness and is not ready for the coming of the lord. Like in *(Revelation 16:15)*, the Church is told here more than once to be watching. Furthermore, Paul clarifies in *(1 Thessalonians 5:4-5)* that we are children of light, and the darkness wouldn't overtake us like the thief. If we stay in our Bibles and follow current events, we will know that the time is drawing nearer, even at the doorstep. Paul also explains Jesus' 2nd coming in terms of birth pangs *(1 Thessalonians 5:3)*. When contractions are minutes apart, you're no longer nine months out; you're in the delivery room. I don't claim to know the day or the hour now, but I know we will soon know the DAY. For example, when the covenant of *Daniel 9:27* is confirmed, we will then know we are within a seven-year timeframe of Jesus' 2nd coming; even with this, you're still left not knowing the exact day or hour. You would think that this event alone would spark an unprecedented urgency among the Church like never before. Like I stated earlier, no one knows the day or hour now, but we who are watching will soon know. It's an event timeline! There are no contradictions. KEEP WATCHING! The WATCHERS are the Church referenced in Revelation 16.

10.

> *4 And I heard another voice from heaven, saying,* **Come out of her, my people***, that ye be not partakers of her sins, and that ye receive not of her plagues. Revelation 18:4 KJV*

There will be some people who will recognize that they are in a false Church or religion led by the False Prophet during the Great Tribulation. They will leave this false religious system before receiving the Mark of the Beast, and they will be saved. God says, *"Come out of her, my people."* This is the Church! This is also evidence of the Great Revival and problems that the true Church causes as a formidable adversary against the Antichrist.

11.

> *6 And I heard as it were the voice of a great multitude, and as the voice of many waters, and as the voice of mighty thunderings, saying, Alleluia: for the Lord God omnipotent reigneth.*
> *7 Let us be glad and rejoice, and give honour to him: for* **the marriage of the Lamb is come***, and* **his wife** *hath made herself ready.*
> *8 And to her was granted that she should be arrayed in fine linen, clean and white: for the fine linen is the righteousness of* **saints***.*
> *9 And he saith unto me, Write, Blessed are they which are called unto* **the marriage supper of the Lamb***. And he saith unto me, These are the true sayings of God. Revelation 19:6-9*

The Marriage of the Lamb has come. "His wife," who is this? It's the Bride. Who is the Bride? It's the Church. We see the Saints mentioned again. Who are the Saints? The Church. Who are the Bride and Saints that get called to the Marriage Supper of the Lamb? It's the Church!

12.

(Revelation 19:14) parallels *(Jude 1:14)*; let's examine both.

> *14 And the **armies** which were in heaven followed him upon white horses, clothed in fine linen, white and clean. Revelation 19:14 KJV*

> *14 And Enoch also, the seventh from Adam, prophesied of these, saying, Behold, the Lord cometh with ten thousands of his **saints**, Jude 1:14 KJV*

In Revelation 19, we learn that the "armies" that follow Jesus are his Saints. Who are his Saints? The Church!

13.

When Jesus comes to receive His bride in the clouds, also known as the 1st resurrection, Jesus will be returning for His Church. This is what the Bible clearly teaches.

> *4 And I saw thrones, and they sat upon them, and judgment was given unto them: and I saw the **souls** of them that were beheaded **for the witness of Jesus**, and for the word of God, and which had not worshipped the beast, neither his image, neither had received his mark upon their foreheads, or in their hands; and **they lived and reigned with Christ a thousand years**. 5 But the rest of the dead lived not again until the thousand years were finished. **This is the <u>first resurrection</u>**. 6 **Blessed and holy is he that hath part in the <u>first resurrection</u>**: on such the second death hath no power, but they shall be priests of God and of Christ, and **shall reign with him a thousand years**. Revelation 20:4-6 KJV*

During the Tribulation, it describes those who died for their faith and those who came through the tribulation as being part of the first resurrection. This first resurrection is the rapture, which occurs after the Great Tribulation. All of which, whether martyred or raptured, being described in this passage, are the Church. There are no 2nd or 3rd, 4th resurrections, etc...... There is only one first resurrection, and it's the Rapture. This didn't happen 7 years prior.

14.

> *2 And I John saw the holy city, **new Jerusalem**, coming down from God out of heaven, prepared as a **bride** adorned for her husband...........9 And there came unto me one of the seven angels which had the seven vials full of the seven last plagues, and talked with me, saying, **Come hither**, I will shew thee the **bride**, the Lamb's wife...........22 And I saw no temple therein: for the Lord God Almighty and **the Lamb are the temple of it**. Revelation 21:2, 9, 22 KJV*

The New Jerusalem is a symbolic representation of the Church, as well as a physical one; however, it lacks a physical temple because Jesus is our temple. Here, we see the phrase "Come hither" once again; John is given a view of the bride 2,000 years before the rapture of the Church, which occurs shortly after the Battle of Armageddon. This is also a picture of Jesus setting up His Kingdom and the transition from human government to a Godly One. The Bride is the Church.

15.

6 And he said unto me, These sayings are faithful and true: and the Lord God of the holy prophets sent his angel to shew unto his servants the things which must shortly be done.
7 **Behold, I come quickly**: *blessed is he that keepeth the sayings of the prophecy of this book.*
8 And I John saw these things, and heard them. And when I had heard and seen, I fell down to worship before the feet of the angel which shewed me these things.
9 Then saith he unto me, See thou do it not: for I am thy fellowservant, and of thy brethren the prophets, and of them which keep the sayings of this book: worship God. 10 And he saith unto me, Seal not the sayings of the prophecy of this book: **for the time is at hand.**
11 He that is unjust, let him be unjust still: and he which is filthy, let him be filthy still: and he that is righteous, let him be righteous still: and he that is holy, let him be holy still.
12 **And, behold, I come quickly; and my reward is with me**, *to give every man according as his work shall be.*
13 I am Alpha and Omega, the beginning and the end, the first and the last.
14 Blessed are they that do his commandments, that they may have right to the tree of life, and may enter in through the gates into the city.
15 For without are dogs, and sorcerers, and whoremongers, and murderers, and idolaters, and whosoever loveth and maketh a lie.
16 I Jesus have sent mine angel to testify unto you these things in the churches. I am the root and the offspring of David, and the bright and morning star. 17 And the Spirit and the **bride** *say, Come. And let him that heareth say, Come. And let him that is athirst come. And whosoever will, let him take the water of life freely.*
18 For I testify unto every man that heareth the words of the prophecy of this book, If any man shall add unto these things, God shall add unto him the plagues that are written in this book:
19 And if any man shall take away from the words of the book of this prophecy, God shall take away his part out of the book of life, and out of the holy city, and from the things which are written in this book.
20 He which testifieth these things saith, **Surely I come quickly.**
Amen. Even so, come, Lord Jesus. 21 The grace of our Lord Jesus Christ be with you all. Amen. Revelation 22:6-21 KJV

(Revelation 22:6-21) The Bride is the Church.

We are now in chapter 22 of Revelation. Jesus repeatedly states that He is coming quickly.

Verse 12, we hear, "Behold, I come quickly, and **My reward** is with me."
We heard this phrase back in Revelation, chapter 11, at the 7th trumpet. This final chapter is yet another account of Jesus' second coming. See now at the many times the Church is mentioned after Revelation 4:1. Now you know why I wasn't able to elaborate earlier in the book about it. The evidence is overwhelming! YES, the Church and the Saints are synonymous with each other!

Wait! I have one more proof. Let's talk about the 144,000.

The 144,000

There are many ideas about who the 144,000 in Revelation actually refer to. Cults have been created throughout modern history, such as the "Jehovah's Witnesses," which centers around the 144,000 of Revelation instead of Jesus and his death, burial, and resurrection. The Bible is very clear on who these people are. We will also discover what exactly this seal is, the timing of the emergence of the sealed 144,000, and the significance this carries prophetically for all Christians.

> *1 And after these things I saw four angels standing on the four corners of the earth, holding the four winds of the earth, that the wind should not blow on the earth, nor on the sea, nor on any tree. 2 And I saw another angel ascending from the east, having **the seal** of the living God: and he cried with a loud voice to the four angels, to whom it was given to hurt the earth and the sea, 3 Saying, Hurt not the earth, neither the sea, nor the trees, till we have **sealed the servants of our God in their foreheads**. 4 And I heard the number of them which were sealed: and there were sealed an **hundred and forty and four thousand of all the tribes of the children of Israel.***
> *Revelation 7:1-4 KJV*

This tells us that the last thing that happens before God pours out His wrath is that He seals the 144,000. Everyone who has given their lives to Christ up until this time, along with these 144,000, is going to be protected from God's wrath.

> *1Then I looked, and behold, **a Lamb standing on Mount Zion, and with Him one hundred and forty-four thousand**, having His **Father's name written on their foreheads**. 2 And I heard a voice from heaven, like the voice of many waters, and like the voice of loud thunder. And I heard the sound of harpists playing their harps. 3 They **sang as it were a new song** before the throne, before the four living creatures, and the elders; and no one could learn that song except the hundred and forty-four*

*thousand **who were redeemed from the earth**. 4 These are the ones who were not defiled with women, for **they are virgins**. These are the ones who follow the Lamb wherever He goes. **These were redeemed** from among men, **being firstfruits** to God and to the Lamb. Revelation 14:1-4 NKJV*

First, we see they are with Jesus on Mount Zion. We will follow up on the significance of that alone in a bit. From this passage, we can gather some other clues about these 144,000:

- **Father's name written on the forehead**
- **They Sing a New Song**
- **Virgins (Spiritually speaking)**
- **They are redeemed (saved)**
- **First Fruits**

Often, you hear that the final seven years are only for the Jews and that the Church will be raptured before the final seven years begin. They would argue that these 144,000 are the ones to evangelize the world after the Church has departed. They place these Messianic Jews in a special box of their own. Though they would disagree, it sounds like a type of replacement theology. Let's pause and take a look at the Church now.

> *27 But there shall by no means enter it anything that defiles, or causes an abomination or a lie, but only **those who are written in the Lamb's Book of Life**. Revelation 21:27 NKJV*

> *4 They shall see His face, and **His name shall be on their foreheads**. Revelation 22:4 NKJV*

When our name is written in the Lamb's book of life, God's name is also written on our foreheads.

> *9 And **they sang a new song**, saying:*
> *"You are worthy to take the scroll,*
> *And to open its seals;*
> *For You were slain,*
> *And have **redeemed** us to God by Your blood*
> ***Out of every tribe and tongue and people and nation**,*
> *10 And have made us kings and priests to our God;*
> *And we shall reign on the earth." Revelation 5:9-10 NKJV*

The Church sings a new song and is redeemed. This isn't the 144,000; this is from every tribe, tongue, peoples, and every nation.

> *2 For I am jealous for you with godly jealousy. For I have betrothed you to one husband, that I may present you as a **chaste virgin to Christ**. 2 Corinthians 11:2 NKJV*

The Church is referred to as a spiritual virgin. Once you have given your life to Christ, it's his blood that is continuously purifying you.

> *18 Of His own will He brought us forth by the word of truth, that we might be a kind of **firstfruits** of His creatures. James 1:18*

The Church is made up of God's first fruits.

Alright! Both groups here have:

- **Father's name in their foreheads**
- **Sing a New Song**
- **Spiritual Virgins**
- **Redeemed**
- **First Fruits unto God**

From this, we know that the 144,000 make up a portion of the Church, and that God has brought them back into the fold of the Church. The 144,000 carry the same exact attributes as the Church holds.

The Rapture of the Church will not happen until the Jews are brought back into the fold of the Church, according to the Bible. Jesus will return for a Jewish/Gentile Church mix just like it was 2,000 years ago. Jesus will return for a complete, beautiful bride, not a partial bride. We as Gentiles serve the God of the Jews, and we will be here right along with them until God finishes the final work of bringing them back into the fold of the Church. How arrogant and unbiblical to say we serve the same God, the Jewish God of the Bible, but that final seven-year thing is only for you Jews for not believing sooner; we as Gentiles will be leaving early. If that doesn't sound like a type of replacement theology that most Christian Churches are teaching right now, then I don't know what is. So, how can I prove this Biblically that both Jews and Gentiles will be here right alongside each other until the literal end?

There is no separation between a Jewish believer and the Church. There is only one plan of salvation and redemption, and the Jews and Gentiles are not in separate boxes in this regard. I submit that the Jews were, in fact, the first members of God's Church, before even the Gentiles. Because the Jews later rejected Jesus, God still has to deal with his chosen people before the millennium kingdom is set up. God will simultaneously deal with the Jewish people and the lukewarm Gentile Church during the final seven years.

> *16 For I am not ashamed of the **gospel of Christ**, for it is the power of God to salvation for **everyone who believes**, for the **Jew first** and also for the **Greek**. Romans 1:16 NKJV*

> *25 For I do not desire, brethren, that you should be ignorant of this mystery, lest you should be wise in your own opinion, that **blindness in part** has happened to Israel **until the fullness of the Gentiles has come in**. 26 And so **all Israel will be saved**, as it is written:"The Deliverer will come out of Zion, And **He will turn away ungodliness from Jacob**; Romans 11:25-26 NKJV*

This verse perfectly describes God simultaneously dealing with the Jews and the Gentiles *(you and me)* during the tribulation. Some Jews will continue to reject Jesus until what the Bible says, "until the fullness of the Gentiles has come in." When this happens, those Jews still alive during the tribulation *(the time of Jacob's trouble, final 3 1/2 years)* will be saved. What does it mean by "until the fullness of the Gentiles come in?" **Answer:** It's when the last Gentile accepts Christ, who is a part of the rapture. The problem with those who say the Gentiles will be raptured before the final seven years is that they must explain why Gentiles will still be saved during the final seven years. We know Christians are here during this time because Revelation refers to them repeatedly throughout as Saints. The fullness of the Gentiles only happens once; God doesn't rapture only Gentile Christians before the final seven years and then say, 'Uh-oh, I forgot a few; I need to save a few more Gentiles during the final seven years.' NO! The reason for "Jacob's Trouble" is to bring the Jews back into the fold of the Church, just like it was 2,000 years ago. Jesus will be coming back for a complete, beautiful bride, not a partial bride.

Let's circle back to Revelation 14, which we looked at earlier.

> *1 Then I looked, and behold, **a Lamb standing on Mount Zion, and with Him one hundred and forty-four thousand,** having **His Father's name written on their foreheads**.*
> *Revelation 14:1*

These 144,000 are with Jesus, standing on Mount Zion. This would be impossible unless they were raptured first. Remember, they carry the same attributes as the Church, and only those with God's name written on their foreheads can be raptured. How do we know they were raptured? Because they are standing on Mount Zion with Jesus.

Mount Zion refers to the new Jerusalem, where Christ will reign on earth after His return. For example:

> *23 Then the moon will be disgraced And the sun ashamed; For the Lord of hosts will reign On **Mount Zion** and in **Jerusalem** And before His elders, **gloriously**. Isaiah 24:23*

> So the Lord will reign over them in **Mount Zion** From now on, even forever. Micah 4:7

This New Jerusalem will come down from heaven to earth.

> ....I will write on him the name of My God and the name of the city of My God, **the New Jerusalem, which comes down out of heaven** from My God. Revelation 3:12

> 2Then I, John, saw the holy city, **New Jerusalem, coming down out of heaven** from God, **prepared as a bride adorned for her husband**. Revelation 21:2

The 144,000 can't be standing with Jesus on Mount Zion, as Revelation Chapter 14 suggests, unless they were raptured. Revelation 21:2 is the drop-the-mike moment. The 144,000 are a part of the bride of Christ, adorned for her husband.

> 9 After these things I looked, and behold, a **great multitude which no one could number**, of all nations, tribes, peoples, and tongues, standing before the throne and before the Lamb, clothed with white robes, with palm branches in their hands, 10 and crying out with a loud voice, saying, "Salvation belongs to our God who sits on the throne, and to the Lamb!"
> Revelation 7:9-10 NKJV

This is a picture of all people from all nations, tribes, peoples, and tongues that no man could number. Who are they?

> 13 Then one of the elders answered, saying to me, "Who are these arrayed in white robes, and where did they come from?" 14 And I said to him, "Sir, you know."
> So he said to me, "**These are the ones who come out of the great tribulation,** and washed their robes and made them white in the blood of the Lamb. Revelation 7:13-14 NKJV

They are they who came out of the Great Tribulation. THE CHURCH! There's going to be the greatest revival this world has ever seen coming shortly, and with urgency, we need not live in fear but instead play our role in this very prophetic time.

Revelation chapter 7 shows us the Jewish church and the Gentile church, out of every nation, tribe, people, and tongue, together right between the 6th and 7th Seals. The timing of the 144,000's revealing is near the end of the tribulation period. The 7th Seal, 7th Trumpet, and 7th Bowl are all the same event —the rapture. Just like the Jews and the Gentiles were together in the early church age. We have discovered that both of these groups are sealed. They are both sealed for the one and only day of redemption, the Rapture.

> *13 In Him you also trusted, after you heard the word of truth,* **the gospel of your salvation;** *in whom also, having believed, you were* **sealed with the Holy Spirit** *of promise, 14 who is the guarantee of our inheritance* **until the redemption of the purchased possession***, to the praise of His glory.*
> Ephesians 1:13-14 NKJV

When you have given your life to Christ after hearing the truth of the gospel that testifies of Jesus, it's at this moment that the Holy Spirit seals you.

> *30 And do not grieve the Holy Spirit of God, by whom* **you were sealed for the day of redemption***.* Ephesians 4:30 NKJV

In both passages, we find that we are sealed unto the day of redemption. The day of redemption takes place only once, when Jesus comes to gather up his undivided Church. The Rapture.

It's by the Holy Spirit that we are raptured. Like the spirit raised Jesus from the grave, we who are in Christ shall be caught up. To teach that the Church will not be here during the Great Tribulation flies directly in the face of what the Bible teaches. If you have read through this book until this point, I hope that I've shown you scripturally why that kind of understanding and teaching is false. Great Scholars have taught that the Church is raptured before the tribulation, therefore, implying the Holy Spirit is removed from the earth, and hence the reason the Antichrist will be able to gain such power and dominance. Yes, he will have much power and dominance; however, we have also learned that he will have resistance. The most vigorous opposition that the Antichrist will have will be the Church! This is not going to be a time of fear but of Faith & Courage to carry out his commandment, the Great Commission, during the Great Tribulation. We need as a Church to be prepared for what lies ahead. Reality will soon set in as events continue to unfold, and the Church, with all these different views, is going to have to get on the same page to be effective during these endtimes. There is only one message of truth that the Bible teaches, and there is only one message of truth that Revelation and other prophetic books of the Bible teach. None contradict each other, instead of searching the scriptures to somehow fit a view that is comfortable to our liking and tickles ours ears. We need to search the scriptures unfiltered to see the truth and then wrap our minds around that. Once we, as a Church, accept the responsibility of the role we are going to play in the last days, it is then that we will see the greatest revival this world has ever had.

I had several questions about all of the things we have discussed at one time in my life. Aren't the Church & Saints the same? Who are the 144,000, and how are they redeemed? What about the two witnesses? Aren't they filled with the Holy Spirit? Wouldn't their ministry be in vain? The Bible says the Antichrist will be making war against the Saints; who are these Saints? What about those who are sealed during the tribulation? Who is the unnumbered multitude that John refers to in heaven that he states came out of the Great Tribulation? The answer I was given was, "Well, after the rapture, there will be some left behind who will have figured it out and decided to give their life to Jesus." I was given this answer, not backed up scripturally at all; It was nothing more than an opinion.

The Holy Spirit is the one who draws us unto God; no one can save themselves. If the Holy Spirit is removed, there is no ministry of the gospel, and there is no means of salvation. The truth is, the Holy Spirit will not be going anywhere during the Great Tribulation. The Church and the Saints are, in fact, synonymous terms. Furthermore, Christ is coming once for his entire Church at the rapture, not multiple times. Jesus will be coming for only those who are sealed by the Holy Spirit. Jesus, when he comes for his Church, will not be leaving anyone behind. If you have not settled the issue of your salvation and relationship with Jesus before he comes to receive his Church, you will not have any second chances.

BE READY!

If a Peace Deal between Israel & Palestinians, along with other nations *(Daniel 9:27)*, is ratified tomorrow by the many (United Nations), we would begin the final seven years to Jesus' return for his Church! Along with recognizing Israel's existence. Here are the Biblical qualifications of the false Peace agreement and why it has to be with the Palestinians.

1) Two-state solution created. Jews will be allowed to live out in the West Bank settlements under Palestinian jurisdiction.

   > *15"Therefore when you see the 'abomination of desolation,' spoken of by Daniel the prophet, standing in the holy place" (whoever reads, let him understand), 16**"then let those who are in Judea flee to the mountains.** Matthew 24:15-16 NKJV*

   Jesus is warning the Jews who live among their enemies in modern-day West Bank to flee at the time of the abomination of desolation. There would be no need to flee if they were living under Israeli jurisdiction.

2) Temple Mount will be supervised under an international sharing arrangement.

   > *1 Then I was given a reed like a measuring rod. And the angel stood, saying, "Rise and measure the temple of God, the altar, and those who worship there. 2 **But leave out the court which is outside the temple, and do not measure it, for it has been given to the Gentiles**. And they will tread the holy city underfoot for forty-two months. Revelation 11:1-2 NKJV*

3) The sharing arrangement will allow Jews to build their 3rd temple, which will be included in the false covenant.

   > *27 Then he shall confirm a covenant with many for one week; But in the middle of the week*
   > ***He shall bring an end to sacrifice and offering.***
   > ***And on the wing of abominations shall be one who makes desolate***, *Even until the consummation, which is determined, Is poured out on the desolate." Daniel 9:27 NKJV*

4) The status of Jerusalem will be put on hold, and Israel will be in control of Jerusalem until the end. You don't invade something you already control.

   > ***2 For I will gather all the nations to battle against Jerusalem**; The city shall be taken, The houses rifled, And the women ravished. Half of the city shall go into captivity, But the remnant of the people shall not be cut off from the city. Zechariah 14:2 NKJV*

So you may be asking yourself, What can I do to prepare myself for everything that is about to unfold? How can I be ready for these endtimes? Should I stock up on food, water, and supplies? There is nothing wrong with preparing for things you know are on the horizon; this is part of the blessing mentioned in Revelation 1:3. In the Bible, God instructed His people to prepare physically for things they were about to encounter many times.

If you're a child of God, the first thing I would suggest to you is not to panic or live in fear. God did not give us a heart of fear.

> *7 For **God has not given us a spirit of fear**, <u>but of power and of love and of a sound mind</u>. 2 Timothy 1:7 NKJV*

The second thing I would suggest is to know your Bible. As Christians, we should be prepared to give an answer. The answers we provide need to be of a Biblical nature. People will seek answers more than ever as events continue to unfold. We need to be people of HOPE.

> *15 But sanctify the Lord God in your hearts: and **be ready always to give an answer to every man that asketh you a reason of the hope that is in you** with meekness and fear: 1 Peter 3:15 KJV*

Daniel, clearly, suggests in the Bible that the Church will have a significant role to play during the end times. How important a role you as an individual will have during the most prophetic time in our world's history since Jesus was on earth 2,000 years ago depends on the first two things we just mentioned. Not living by fear but by the power who resides in you and by being a person of HOPE for a lost world seeking answers.

> *..but the people that do know their God **shall be strong, and do exploits**. 33 And **they that understand among the people shall instruct many**...Daniel 11:32-33 KJV*

If you are someone who has read this book seeking answers but doesn't have a relationship with Jesus, my plea for you to "Be Ready" for what lies ahead is to not wait until tomorrow to settle the issue of your salvation. No one is promised tomorrow. As you've learned, once you have given your life to Jesus Christ, you are sealed with the Holy Spirit and forever protected. It's not about religion, it's about a relationship.

- First, you must realize you are a sinner in need of a savior. You must acknowledge your sinful condition and understand that Jesus alone is your only solution.

    23 for all have sinned and fall short of the glory of God, Romans 3:23 NKJV

    23 For the wages of sin is death, but the gift of God is eternal life in Christ Jesus our Lord. Romans 6:23 NKJV

- Second, you must believe that Jesus died on the cross for your sins and rose the 3rd day from the dead as victory over your sin.

    *16 For God so loved the world that He gave His only begotten Son, that whoever **believes in Him** should not perish but have everlasting life. 17 For God did not send His Son into the world to condemn the world, but that the world through Him might be saved. John 3:16-17 NKJV*

- Third, you need to confess that you're a sinner to Jesus himself and ask him to come into your life to be Lord, Savior, and Ruler.

    9 that if you confess with your mouth the Lord Jesus and believe in your heart that God has raised Him from the dead, you will be saved. 10 For with the heart one believes unto righteousness, and with the mouth confession is made unto salvation. **Romans 10:9-10 NKJV**

You could pray something like this in your own words, straight from your heart.

Lord Jesus, I know that I'm a sinner, and I ask for forgiveness of my sins. I believe you died on the cross and rose on the third day so I could receive your forgiveness and eternal life. I ask that you come into my life and guide me. I give you control over my life and ask that you help me live for you from this day forward. Amen.

If you have just given your life to Jesus Christ, your name is written in the Lamb's Book of Life, His Holy Spirit has sealed you for eternity, and the angels in heaven are rejoicing now over your decision. You are now READY!

   10 Likewise, I say to you, there is joy in the presence of the angels of God over one sinner who repents." Luke 15:10 NKJV

Your Purpose in life is simple: don't live by fear; instead, go out as the victorious Christian you are and be the light of Christ in this dark world for everyone around you to see. For Jesus is coming soon!

> 14 **"You are the light of the world.** *A city that is set on a hill cannot be hidden.* 15 *Nor do they light a lamp and put it under a basket, but on a lampstand, and it gives light to all who are in the house.* 16 **Let your light so shine before men,** *that they may see your good works and glorify your Father in heaven.*
> Matthew 5:14-16 NKJV

Find yourself a Bible-believing Church for community. Although baptism is not a requirement for salvation, it's considered a first act of obedience to Christ as a believer. It symbolizes, much like a wedding band, that you now have a relationship with Jesus; your baptism also serves as a great witness for those who are lost. Jesus was baptized and asked us to be baptized as well.

No one is promised tomorrow, and the doctrine of imminence applies only in that regard. Today is indeed the day of Salvation. As we continue to see God's prophetic word being fulfilled, it is this that will strengthen the Church's faith and provide the urgency of preparing herself as the Bride adorned for her bridegroom. Being a pre-trib person all my life, this was a harder pill to swallow; however, the prophetic scriptures and the gospel do not contradict each other, and the truth is what matters. Knowledge is power, and by knowing these things, we are provided with the advantage of knowing what's coming so that we can be prepared mentally, emotionally, physically, and spiritually. Jesus will not be coming back for a beaten bride but a "spiritually" beautiful bride! The greatest revival the world has ever seen will occur before Christ's return (Matthew 24:13-14). The Good News is, Jesus is coming soon, and it will not be long! Be Ready!

John 14:29

God chose you to live through this Biblically prophetic time in history for his glory! He wouldn't have allowed you to be born during these times that will soon lead to his return if he didn't think you were capable of shining for him. He sees greatness in you! He sees greatness in the remnant of his Church!

C. S. DeCaro

I'm an independently published author who needs a little help getting the word out. One easy way to help inform and prepare the Church for the times in which we live is to take one minute to copy and paste an Amazon link of this book to your social media pages.

It doesn't end here. Want to receive Bible Prophecy Updates as events continue to unfold? Join my SUBSTACK publication as a FREE or donating subscriber today! Tell a friend!

SUBSCRIBE HERE!

Books Available In Paperback & E-book

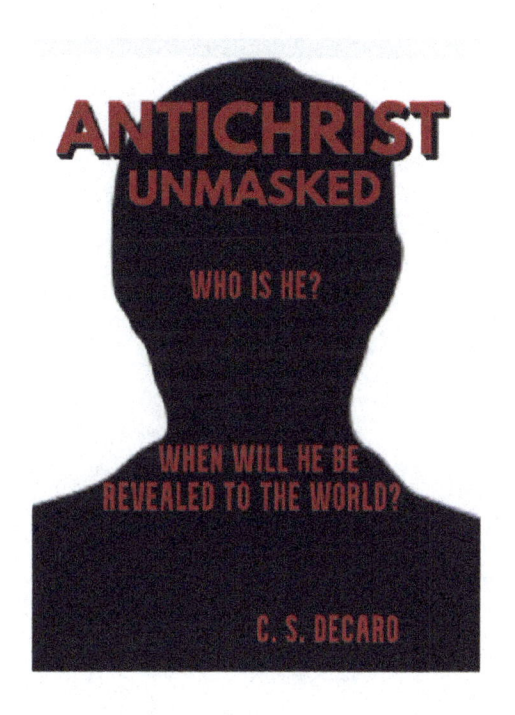

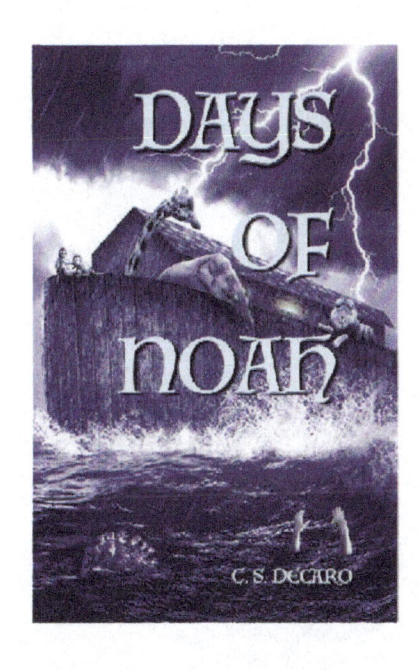

BIBLIOGRAPHY

King James Version Bible, KJV

New King James Version Bible, NKJV

New Revised Standard Version Bible, NRSV

https://www.bible.com Bible App (It's Free)

Endtime Ministries

Vatican City | History, Map, Flag, & Facts | Britannica. https://www.britannica.com/place/Vatican-City Britannica

https://www.britannica.com/event/Chernobyl-disaster Chernobyl, Britannica

https://www.washingtonpost.com/archive/politics/2006/01/26/al-gore-sundances-leading-man-span-classbankheadan-inconvenient-truth-documents-his-efforts-to-raise-alarm-on-effects-of-global-warmingspan/2929bc60-5260-4f89-8bb9-ffade9473807/ Washington Post, January 26, 2006

https://www.faf.ae/home/2024/11/23/what-led-to-erdogan-cutting-water-supply-to-millions-of-kurds Other News 11/11/2019

https://www.newworldencyclopedia.org/entry/Holy_Roman_Empire New World Encyclopedia

https://www.britannica.com/event/Lisbon-Treaty Britannica

https://www.history.com/topics/middle-ages/charlemagne History June 6, 2019

https://www.ecfr.eu/publications/summary/can_europe_save_the_world_order Can Europe Save the World Order?

https://peoplesdispatch.org/2020/08/24/uae-israel-deal-is-yet-another-dagger-in-palestines-back/ Reference to Fig Leaf Comments

https://www.marketwatch.com/story/states-are-cracking-down-on-companies-microchipping-their-employees-how-common-is-it-and-why-does-it-happen-2020-02-03 Market Watch February 4, 2020

https://nypost.com/2019/07/14/swedish-people-are-getting-chip-implants-to-replace-cash-credit-cards/ New York Post, July 14, 2019
https://www.techpolicy.press/public-infrastructure-and-private-surveillance-in-indias-aadhaar-system/ India's Aadhaar

https://www.biometricupdate.com/201909/id2020-and-partners-launch-program-to-provide-digital-id-with-vaccines Biometric update, September 20, 2019

https://images.app.goo.gl/6ccegLWCcTg5vMECA Earth from space, Labeled for reuse

"sky" by walmarc04 is licensed under CC PDM 1.0

"bald eagle Maymont Park Richmond Va." by watts_photos is licensed under CC PDM 1.0

"File:Lone Rooster.jpg" by Jean Beaufort is licensed under CC0 1.0

"Leopard Tank" by South Australian History Network is licensed under CC0 1.0

"Flag of Israel" by Alex Fox is licensed under CC0 1.0

"File:China flag icon.png" by Gb89.2 is licensed under CC0 1.0

"Soviet Flag" by Gary Lee Todd, Ph.D. is licensed under CC0 1.0

"court" is licensed under CC0 1.0

https://branham.org/articles/9222015_VicarOfChrist Triple Crown

https://images.app.goo.gl/rFFgTUsWc7nNQwLb6 Flag of Muslim League, labeled for reuse

https://images.app.goo.gl/B3YC2utRCZGjA4sZ9 Digital collections of the National WW2 Museum

https://images.app.goo.gl/cx3HxBAbJmtNgnwP6 Chernobyl angel, labeled for reuse

https://images.app.goo.gl/nXhPQznoLYxndHCp6 Chernobyl radiation map, labeled for reuse

"The fall of the Berlin Wall - November 1989" by gavinandrewstewart is licensed under CC BY 2.0

https://images.app.goo.gl/wLGiwpvw3rSE4k8G7 Kuwait oil fires, Labeled for reuse

https://images.app.goo.gl/hNngAcJQzFRgTkDJ6 Planes, Kuwait oil fires, Labeled for reuse https://www.toledoblade.com/image/2003/04/08/800x_b1_cCM_z/IRAQ-WAR-OIL.jpg Helicopter, oil fires

https://images.app.goo.gl/EvxTSqqCA6PBoiRQ7 Vatican City, Labeled for reuse

https://images.app.goo.gl/fY3FU8nKUXWNxvz19 Ataturk Dam. NPR

https://i.pinimg.com/originals/34/26/08/342608017fef0924b7711d87cda87d2d.jpg WW1 throwing bombs from plane

⚠

Graphic Content Website

This website contains extremely difficult to watch content from the terrible massacre carried out by Hamas on the seventh of October

Link: October 7th Attacks Against Israel

Made in the USA
Coppell, TX
06 November 2025